SUICIDE
OPPOSING VIEWPOINTS®

Other Books of Related Interest in the Opposing
Viewpoints Series:

AIDS
American Values
Biomedical Ethics
Constructing a Life Philosophy
Death and Dying
The Elderly
Euthanasia
Religion in America
Science and Religion

SUICIDE

OPPOSING VIEWPOINTS®

David L. Bender & Bruno Leone, *Series Editors*

Michael Biskup, *Book Editor*
Carol Wekesser, *Assistant Editor*

OPPOSING VIEWPOINTS SERIES ®

Greenhaven Press, Inc.   PO Box 289009   San Diego, CA 92198-9009

Library of Congress Cataloging-in-Publication Data

Suicide : opposing viewpoints / Michael Biskup, book editor, & Carol Wekesser, assistant editor
    p.   cm.—(Opposing viewpoints series)
    Includes bibliographical references and index.
    Summary: Presents opposing viewpoints on various aspects of suicide, including individual rights, physician-assisted suicide, and prevention.
    ISBN 0-89908-193-2 (lib.: alk. paper).—ISBN 0-89908-168-1 (pbk. : alk. paper).
    1. Suicide—United States. 2. Suicide—Moral and ethical aspects. 3. Teenagers—United States—Suicidal behavior.
[1. Suicide.] I. Biskup, Michael, 1956-   . II. Wekesser, Carol, 1963- . III. Series (Unnumbered)
HV6548.U5S86 1992
362.2'8'0973—dc20   92-6093
                                      CIP
                                       AC

"Congress shall make no law . . .
abridging the freedom of speech,
or of the press."

First Amendment to the U.S. Constitution

The basic foundation of our democracy is the first amendment
guarantee of freedom of expression. The Opposing Viewpoints
Series is dedicated to the concept of this basic freedom and the
idea that it is more important to practice it than to enshrine it.

Contents

Page

Why Consider Opposing Viewpoints?   9

Introduction   13

Chapter 1: Is Suicide an Individual Right?

Chapter Preface   16
1. Suicide Is an Individual Right   17
   Richard W. Momeyer

2. Suicide Is Not an Individual Right   24
   Victor G. Rosenblum & Clarke D. Forsythe

3. Suicide Can Be a Rational Choice   31
   Alan W. Johnson

4. Suicide Can Never Be a Rational Choice   38
   Leon R. Kass

A Critical Thinking Activity:
   The Ability to Empathize   44
Periodical Bibliography   47

Chapter 2: Should Physicians Assist Terminally
           Ill Patients in Suicide?

Chapter Preface   49
1. Physicians Can Ethically Assist in Suicide   51
   Sidney H. Wanzer et al.

2. Physicians Cannot Ethically Assist in Suicide   57
   David Orentlicher

3. Physician-Assisted Suicide Should Be Legal   62
   Jack Kevorkian

4. Physician-Assisted Suicide Should Not Be Legal   69
   Daniel Callahan

A Critical Thinking Activity:
   Understanding Words in Context   76
Periodical Bibliography   78

Chapter 3: What Are the Causes of Teen Suicide?

Chapter Preface 80

1. Stress Causes Teen Suicide 81
   Judith M. Stillion, Eugene E. McDowell &
   Jacque H. May

2. Guns in the Home Cause Teen Suicide 88
   David A. Brent et al.

3. Alcohol and Drug Abuse Causes Teen Suicide 94
   Marc A. & Judith J. Schuckit

4. Society's Rejection of Homosexual Teens Causes
   Suicide 100
   Paul Gibson

5. The Decline of Religion and Family Causes Teen
   Suicide 108
   Allan C. Carlson

6. There Is No Single Cause of Teen Suicide 114
   George Howe Colt

A Critical Thinking Activity:
   Distinguishing Between Fact and Opinion 121

Periodical Bibliography 123

Chapter 4: How Can Suicide Be Prevented?

Chapter Preface 125

1. Suicide Prevention Centers Can Help Prevent
   Suicide 127
   George Howe Colt

2. Education Can Help Prevent Suicide 135
   Judith M. Stillion, Eugene E. McDowell &
   Jacque H. May

3. The Media Can Help Prevent Suicide 143
   Alan L. Berman

4. Changes in Society Can Help Prevent Suicide 151
   David Lester

5. Intervention by Friends Can Help Prevent Suicide 158
   Suicide Prevention and Crisis Center of San Mateo
   County, California

6. Improving the Lives of the Elderly Can Prevent
   Suicide   162
        Alexander C. Morgan
   A Critical Thinking Activity:
        Evaluating Suicide Education Courses   170
   Periodical Bibliography   173

Organizations to Contact   174
Annotated Book Bibliography   180
Index   185

Why Consider Opposing Viewpoints?

"It is better to debate a question without settling it than to settle a question without debating it."

Joseph Joubert (1754-1824)

The Importance of Examining Opposing Viewpoints

The purpose of the Opposing Viewpoints Series, and this book in particular, is to present balanced, and often difficult to find, opposing points of view on complex and sensitive issues.

Probably the best way to become informed is to analyze the positions of those who are regarded as experts and well studied on issues. It is important to consider every variety of opinion in an attempt to determine the truth. Opinions from the mainstream of society should be examined. But also important are opinions that are considered radical, reactionary, or minority as well as those stigmatized by some other uncomplimentary label. An important lesson of history is the eventual acceptance of many unpopular and even despised opinions. The ideas of Socrates, Jesus, and Galileo are good examples of this.

Readers will approach this book with their own opinions on the issues debated within it. However, to have a good grasp of one's own viewpoint, it is necessary to understand the arguments of those with whom one disagrees. It can be said that those who do not completely understand their adversary's point of view do not fully understand their own.

A persuasive case for considering opposing viewpoints has been presented by John Stuart Mill in his work *On Liberty*. When examining controversial issues it may be helpful to reflect on this suggestion:

The only way in which a human being can make some approach to knowing the whole of a subject, is by hearing what can be said about it by persons of every variety of opinion, and studying all modes in which it can be looked at by every character of mind. No wise man ever acquired his wisdom in any mode but this.

Analyzing Sources of Information

The Opposing Viewpoints Series includes diverse materials taken from magazines, journals, books, and newspapers, as well as statements and position papers from a wide range of individuals, organizations, and governments. This broad spectrum of sources helps to develop patterns of thinking which are open to the consideration of a variety of opinions.

Pitfalls to Avoid

A pitfall to avoid in considering opposing points of view is that of regarding one's own opinion as being common sense and the most rational stance, and the point of view of others as being only opinion and naturally wrong. It may be that another's opinion is correct and one's own is in error.

Another pitfall to avoid is that of closing one's mind to the opinions of those with whom one disagrees. The best way to approach a dialogue is to make one's primary purpose that of understanding the mind and arguments of the other person and not that of enlightening him or her with one's own solutions. More can be learned by listening than speaking.

It is my hope that after reading this book the reader will have a deeper understanding of the issues debated and will appreciate the complexity of even seemingly simple issues on which good and honest people disagree. This awareness is particularly important in a democratic society such as ours where people enter into public debate to determine the common good. Those with whom one disagrees should not necessarily be regarded as enemies, but perhaps simply as people who suggest different paths to a common goal.

Developing Basic Reading and Thinking Skills

In this book, carefully edited opposing viewpoints are purposely placed back to back to create a running debate; each viewpoint is preceded by a short quotation that best expresses the author's main argument. This format instantly plunges the reader into the midst of a controversial issue and greatly aids that reader in mastering the basic skill of recognizing an author's point of view.

A number of basic skills for critical thinking are practiced in the activities that appear throughout the books in the series. Some of the skills are:

Evaluating Sources of Information. The ability to choose from among alternative sources the most reliable and accurate source in relation to a given subject.

Separating Fact from Opinion. The ability to make the basic distinction between factual statements (those that can be demonstrated or verified empirically) and statements of opinion (those that are beliefs or attitudes that cannot be proved).

Identifying Stereotypes. The ability to identify oversimplified, exaggerated descriptions (favorable or unfavorable) about people and insulting statements about racial, religious, or national groups, based upon misinformation or lack of information.

Recognizing Ethnocentrism. The ability to recognize attitudes or opinions that express the view that one's own race, culture, or group is inherently superior, or those attitudes that judge another culture or group in terms of one's own.

It is important to consider opposing viewpoints and equally important to be able to critically analyze those viewpoints. The activities in this book are designed to help the reader master these thinking skills. Statements are taken from the book's viewpoints and the reader is asked to analyze them. This technique aids the reader in developing skills that not only can be applied to the viewpoints in this book, but also to situations where opinionated spokespersons comment on controversial issues. Although the activities are helpful to the solitary reader, they are most useful when the reader can benefit from the interaction of group discussion.

Using this book and others in the series should help readers develop basic reading and thinking skills. These skills should improve the reader's ability to understand what is read. Readers should be better able to separate fact from opinion, substance from rhetoric, and become better consumers of information in our media-centered culture.

This volume of the Opposing Viewpoints Series does not advocate a particular point of view. Quite the contrary! The very nature of the book leaves it to the reader to formulate the opinions he or she finds most suitable. My purpose as publisher is to see that this is made possible by offering a wide range of viewpoints that are fairly presented.

David L. Bender
Publisher

Introduction

"The man who voluntarily kills himself in anger does an act contrary to a just law."

Aristotle, *Nicomachean Ethics*

"Just as I shall select my ship when I am about to go on a voyage, or my house when I propose to take a residence, so I shall choose my death when I am about to depart from life."

Seneca, *Epistulae Morales*

For most of the last fifteen hundred years, much of Western civilization considered suicide an immoral act committed by the sinful or insane. This view, an outgrowth of Christianity, began to spread across Europe as the new religion took root in the first centuries after Christ. Although the Bible says little about suicide specifically, Christian authorities interpreted the biblical commandment "Thou shalt not kill" as a prohibition against suicide.

By the Middle Ages, the tenets of the Catholic church dominated Western thought. These tenets held killing oneself to be one of the few sins that guaranteed everlasting condemnation in hell. Thirteenth-century theologian St. Thomas Aquinas stated this view in his work *Summa Theologica:* "Whoever takes his own life, sins against God. . . . For it belongs to God alone to pronounce sentence of life and death." Not only was suicide considered a mortal sin, many people also believed it to be a sign of insanity or satanic possession. "All persons who kill themselves are impotent in mind," philosopher Benedict de Spinoza wrote in 1677.

This view of suicide remained unchallenged for hundreds of years. Suicide was considered such a taboo that there was little if any debate concerning its morality until the Enlightenment of the eighteenth century, when a few philosophers, such as David Hume, challenged the taboo. Hume believed that the free will that God gave humans included the freedom to take one's life. This was especially true, Hume argued, when life became un-

13

bearable: "That suicide may often be consistent with interest and with our duty to *ourselves*, no one can question, who allows that age, sickness, or misfortune may render life a burden, and make it worse even than annihilation."

Although Hume's view remains in the minority to this day, it has gained more prominence. Now that physicians can prolong the lives of dying patients, sometimes beyond the point at which life has value, some people end up living in vegetative states, or physically or mentally unable to care for themselves. These people become a burden to their families and society. Some of these patients have turned to suicide as a way to end their pain and hasten their deaths.

Advocates for the terminally ill have established organizations such as The Hemlock Society to assist the dying in committing suicide. In the United States, the right-to-die movement has spurred groups in several states to hold public initiatives to legalize physician-assisted suicide. These initiatives have been extremely controversial, with opponents arguing that legalizing physician-assisted suicide is tantamount to legalizing murder, and that the end result will be an epidemic of suicide and the wanton killing of the weak, ill, and disabled.

Suicide: Opposing Viewpoints addresses these issues and others in the following chapters: Is Suicide an Individual Right? Should Physicians Assist Terminally Ill Patients in Suicide? What Are the Causes of Teen Suicide? How Can Suicide Be Prevented? Suicide is a highly emotional issue. By reading the viewpoints in this book, the editors hope the reader will gain a more thorough understanding of the controversies surrounding this sensitive topic.

Is Suicide an Individual Right?

Chapter Preface

The November 4, 1989 issue of the *New York Times* related the story of an eighty-three-year-old widow whose health was declining rapidly after major surgery. Because of blocked arteries, the widow was vulnerable to a stroke that could either kill her or leave her mentally incompetent. Since she could not justify becoming a burden to herself or to anyone in her family, she began contemplating suicide. While the widow's ultimate decision is never revealed, her story is similar to the stories of many Americans whose severe illnesses lead them to weigh a future filled with pain against the option of suicide. This issue has come to be known as the right-to-die debate.

Right-to-die proponents contend that it respects individual freedom and dignity. In a speech before the Forum of Medical Affairs, Eva M. Skinner of the American Association of Retired Persons said, "Dignity comes with our ability to maintain control over our bodies." Advocates believe suicide can be a rational choice when weighed against the prospects of a life that involves pain and suffering which medical treatment cannot alleviate. In an editorial to the *San Diego Tribune*, Richard Stratton notes that "The right to a 'good death' when the quality has been shattered beyond repair is not only important, but is vital. A law establishing that right would be the hallmark of an advanced, rational, and compassionate civilization." Proponents support the establishment of laws that would respect an individual's right to die.

Those who oppose passing such laws believe that people who are terminally ill and want to die are deeply depressed and require help. In a December 4, 1991, *New York Times* article, Dr. David C. Clark of the American Association of Suicidology is quoted as saying, "A person who is severely depressed can't think rationally about suicide. When he says he wants to kill himself, that's the depression talking, compromising his judgment." The studies from this article point out that those who face death from illness and who contemplate suicide are reaching out for help and can be treated for their depression. Opponents contend that laws establishing the right to die would encourage the elderly or terminally ill to commit suicide to avoid being an emotional and financial burden to their family or society.

The issue of an individual right to die sparks a debate that forces society to reevaluate its views on suicide and how these beliefs affect its acceptance today. The following articles focus on this issue.

===

"There is a right to choose death."

===

Suicide Is an Individual Right

Richard W. Momeyer

Richard W. Momeyer believes that individuals can make a rational choice to die. In the following viewpoint, he contends that society should encourage the sick and dying to live, but it should not interfere with a person who chooses to die. He argues that the right to die is an expression of freedom that each person possesses. Society should respect the dignity of the individual by allowing him or her to commit suicide. Momeyer, a professor at Miami University near Cincinnati, Ohio, writes and lectures about the individual's right to choose when to die.

As you read, consider the following questions:

1. If a right to suicide existed, why does Momeyer believe there would have to be changes in legal and social institutions?
2. Why does the author reject the idea of human lives being property?
3. According to Momeyer, what specific actions should society take to help those who wish to die?

Excerpted from Richard W. Momeyer, *Confronting Death.* Bloomington: Indiana University Press, 1988. Reprinted with permission.

The right to die is asserted in the context of someone's dying, where death is imminent and unavoidable. What is wanted is a specification of what rights a dying person has to exercise some measure of control over her or his dying. But with the assertion of "a right to choose death" or "a right to suicide," something far more radical is being claimed, namely, that one has a right to choose death even when not dying. Much more is at stake than control over the conditions of dying; what is at stake is nothing less than whether one has, as a matter of moral right and potentially legal privilege, sanction "to take arms against a sea of troubles, and by opposing end them" (Hamlet).

Right to Choose

To adopt the point of view that individuals possess a right to choose death by self-inflicted means is a considerable change of perspective from still conventional attitudes. Among other things, it would shift the burden of moral criticism from those who attempt or succeed in suicide to those who would intervene to prevent such efforts. If there is a right to suicide, then interference with the exercise of that right is *prima facie* wrong, and always in need of justification. The exercise of one's rights is conversely *prima facie* right, and needs no justification until challenged. Further, numerous alterations in law and social institutions would be required in order to recognize this right. Police, psychiatrists, hospitals of all sorts, insurance companies, crisis intervention centers, prisons, and the military would all be enormously affected. But if there is a good case for a right to suicide, then the changes in public attitudes leading to sweeping changes in law, public policy, and institutional structures would all be for the better.

Three Conditions

Three rather different grounds might be advanced in support of the claim to a right to suicide. These are (1) that each person's life belongs to oneself alone and, like other property, may be disposed of as the owner pleases; (2) that making such choices is an exercise of autonomy by competent moral agents and that such choices require the same respect as any other choice made by such persons; or (3) that making such choices as for one's own death is among the fundamental human rights that should be recognized as belonging to every human being. The first two of these grounds for a right to suicide suppose that such a right is directly derivative from a fundamental human right—to property, or for freedom; the third claims that choosing death is itself as fundamental a human right as property or freedom, that it needs no derivation or qualification as a second-order right. There are both arguments for and difficulties with each of these foundations for a right to suicide.

On this view, each person is regarded as having a unique relationship to his or her own life, one that might be called "nontransferable ownership." Our lives are our property, and, while a kind of property that cannot be given over to another, they are, like other property, something over which we have the right of disposition. . . .

Objections to this way of grounding a right to suicide are legion, the most familiar no doubt being a direct challenge to the presumption that each of us owns our life. Rather, it is claimed, our lives are "owned" by God, who lends them to us, or by the state, to whom we owe primary allegiance. Various Judaic-Christian theologies have maintained the former; the latter goes back at least to Plato and Aristotle. Notice that this is a disagreement simply about property *rights* and not about property; that is, it does not challenge the notion that human life can intelligibly and properly be regarded as property. . . .

Don Wright/*The Palm Beach Post*. Reprinted with permission.

There is something quite demeaning to persons in the view that the interest we have in our very lives is anything like the interest we have in property. A grandiose way of saying this is that property is simply not a concept of sufficient ontological status to encompass human life. A more modest way is to say that we diminish the significance and value of human beings when we reduce the regard each of us has for our life to that which we might have for our car, or TV, or shoes. The value of human life is greater than any concept of property can incorporate. It is one of the perversions of a culture so enamored of material possessions and "property rights" that we would even for a moment suppose that something elevating was being claimed for persons when it is said that each of us has a right to dispose of our life as we see fit because it is our property. . . .

Conditions to Suicide

A right to suicide can be regarded as derivative from the fundamental right of self-determination. For those persons who see it as in their best interest to die, who freely choose this and pursue it, respect is owed. That respect must be shown by the rest of us in the form of noninterference with their pursuit of what they have chosen. In showing such respect, we are but abiding by the fundamental obligation to respect the autonomous choices of others entailed by the Principle of Autonomy. . . .

Suicide is an act that does not occur in a vacuum, and it is ordinarily not without very serious and often devastating consequences for others. Even if it can be claimed as a right, it is not inappropriate that one be very careful to assure that exercising that right is the right thing to do. Having a right to do something provides us some entitlement to do it; it does not assure that doing it is right. It is appropriate to set very high standards of justification for exercising a right to suicide, given how often it is undertaken in an ill-considered manner, how frequently suiciders suffer diminished competence from mental illness, and how widespread and serious are the consequences for others. . . .

I am inclined to think that a right to suicide and its justification are better expressed as follows. There is a right to choose death when, and only when, doing so is the expression or enhancement of a person's human dignity. Choosing death is most likely to be such an expression in those nonhostile choices for death labeled euthanatic, self-sacrificing, and protest. We have a right to make such choices as a function of our right to live with dignity. This right, in turn, derives from our fundamental right to live and a theory of justice that specifies the minimal conditions necessary for each of us to attain life with dignity. . . .

I think there is a right to kill oneself, but only when doing so serves human dignity. I do not think such a right is, in the fullest sense, "fundamental." I do think, however, it is very extensive, more so even than such a right would be if it were simply a "liberty" right. . . .

A community that values its members does not respond to their most extreme sufferings by suggesting that they would be better off dead—even if this is true. Rather, it is incumbent upon each of us to do all in our power to mitigate that suffering, in every way short of killing or encouraging self-killing. The very best part of the dominant religious traditions in Western societies has always been the insistence upon creating a community that minimizes injustice and suffering, but holds that where such creeps in it must be spread about and shared. Not all suffering is meaningful; no good will or can result from it. But all suffering can be shared in some fashion. Notions of abiding with others and suffering together seem a much more humane and dignified response to hardship than assurances that it is permissible, and even the exercise of a basic human right, to kill oneself. In such a society, our resources for ameliorating suffering would be invested in hospices and not in ethical suicide parlors.

Denying Individual Liberty

Since suicide is an exercise and expression of human freedom, it can be prevented only by curtailing human freedom. This is why deprivation of liberty becomes, in institutional psychiatry, a form of treatment. . . .

Whether those who curtail other people's liberties act with complete sincerity, or with utter cynicism, hardly matters. What matters is what happens: the abridgment of individual liberty, justified, in the case of suicide prevention, by psychiatric rhetoric.

Thomas S. Szasz in *Suicide: Right or Wrong?*, 1990.

The objection here is not a slippery slope argument that by recognizing a right to choose death we will eventually arrive at a much worse society for everyone. Rather, it is an objection to communicating to people, in a social context, that others believe the most adequate response to their suffering is that they die, even if by their own hand. This seems to be in principle the wrong message to give another, suffering human being. It would be far better that our concern be expressed as a willingness on our part to share the burden of suffering, however we might, short of promoting the desirability of death.

But it may be that this is really an objection to no more than others *initiating* consideration of death as the escape from unwanted life. Suppose one were only responding to such a proposal from someone who felt their life was not worth going on with? Should the response be sympathetic and supportive, because the other person is simply considering exercising her or his rights?

I don't see that the issues are any different in responding to

21

another's consideration of choosing death than they are if we ourselves initiate such consideration by promoting choices for death as a matter of right and the exercise of dignity. It is still the case that in the most fully human community it would be better to nurture hope for meaningful life and share the burden of making life worthwhile than it would be to encourage an option to take a shortcut through this struggle to death. In either case, we would be failing in our duty to sustain one another in times of crisis, and failing to create the conditions of social existence within which alone human life can be worthwhile.

Like the other reservations about regarding choices for death as a fundamental human right, this one is more cautionary than decisive. Human dignity may be a tenuous basis on which to found all human rights, but there is no denying that it is vitally important, somehow connected to any notion of rights, and a compelling consideration in assessing the propriety of any choice for death. Suicide may only sometimes be "constitutive" of human dignity, but in those cases in which it is, there is more than merely adequate reason to respect someone's choice to elect death by self-inflicted means. And now here, while acknowledging, even encouraging a right to choose death may not be the appropriate first (or even second) response of a decent community, there is no good reason to think it an improper response in the right circumstances and at the right time. . . .

Finding a Balance

In another sense, the task is to find that balance between elevating individual choice to the point where community is rendered impossible, and denying persons the exercise of their rights because allowing such is regarded as not good for them or for others. With respect to suicide, it is surely desirable to eliminate the social stigma that presently attaches to nearly all suicide and move a great ways toward a more tolerant, even respectful understanding of what motivates those drawn to self-destruction in a wide variety of circumstances. But it cannot be desirable to move so far as to give open-ended permission, even encouragement, to persons in all or even very dire circumstances to exercise a right to die. A decent society finds ways of caring for those even in the most extreme distress; rarely is it the case that such caring is best done by encouraging death, through either suicide or euthanasia. Rarely, I said, but not never. For neither is it the case that in a decent society we would burden those for whom death is in their best interest with the sole responsibility for ending their lives, any more than we burden everyone with sole responsibility for sustaining their lives when this is best. . . .

In the final analysis, we do not serve the cause of ensuring human dignity by social mechanisms for making death easy and painless, by promoting self-inflicted and socially encouraged death for those whose ongoing lives are burdensome to themselves or others, any more than we respect dignity when we go to great and repressive lengths to prevent all suicide and every other means of choosing death.

We need to guard against the illusions that prevent clear vision about suicide as much as about other forms of death. It will not do to romanticize suicide as a rational, desirable, rightful choice—even though it can be all these things. . . .

A Matter of Human Rights

I believe people have a right to decide, for a vast variety of reasons and in highly diverse circumstances, that their lives are not worth continuing. I believe further that they frequently have the right to act accordingly on such assessments and end life. Sometimes these decisions and actions are not simply an exercise of a right; they are the right decisions and actions.

The right each of us has to choose death is a right bred both by the entitlement to liberty each possesses as an autonomous person deserving moral respect and, still more fundamentally, by the requirements of human dignity itself. Not much suicide is an expression or enhancement of human dignity, but that which is occurs as a matter of human right, a right derived from considerations of justice and our fundamental right to live with dignity.

Recognition of such a right raises very difficult questions about the proper response of other members of a community to the exercise of the right. The first obligation would seem to be to shed whatever moralistic prejudices we retain about the wrongness of suicide. The second is not thereby to approve all suicide and set about making those changes in law, medicine, and social institutions required to facilitate suicide. Rather, I have argued, the better course is to evaluate carefully each would-be suicide's ostensible desire for death to see if it is genuine and supported by compelling reasons.

Even after this is done, however, there is much more that a decent community would do to try to share its concerns and resources with those persons wanting to leave it forever. These range from suicide prevention centers (whose powers do not exceed the limits of respecting the freedom and dignity of competent persons), to imaginative ways of relieving another's suffering through sharing, to hospices. As with those drawn to suicide, for whatever reasons in whatever circumstances, those who live on must seek to expand stultified imagination in finding modes of caring sufficient to deter a choice for death. Only as a last resort, after all other forms of caring have failed, does respect for another's right to choose death obligate us not to interfere, and sometimes to assist.

23

"There is no 'right' to do what is intrinsically wrong, and Anglo-American law . . . [holds] suicide to be intrinsically wrong."

Suicide Is Not an Individual Right

Victor G. Rosenblum and Clarke D. Forsythe

In the following viewpoint, Victor G. Rosenblum and Clarke D. Forsythe state that suicide is not an individual right under the U.S. Constitution. They believe suicide is wrong and that society should work to prevent suicide and to reach out to those who are depressed and suicidal. Rosenblum is professor of law at Northwestern University, and Forsythe is general counsel for the Americans United for Life Legal Defense Fund (AUL), both located in Chicago.

As you read, consider the following questions:

1. Why do Rosenblum and Forsythe say the term "right to die" is incorrectly used?
2. Why do the authors believe suicide is wrong?
3. According to Rosenblum and Forsythe, what are the consequences if society accepts suicide as a right?

From Victor G. Rosenblum and Clarke D. Forsythe, "The Right to Assisted Suicide: Protection of Autonomy or an Open Door to Social Killing?" Reprinted by permission of the publisher, *Issues in Law & Medicine*, vol. 6, no. 1, Summer 1990. Copyright © 1990 by the National Legal Center for the Medically Dependent & Disabled, Inc.

The current campaign for the legalization of assisted suicide runs directly counter to the long history of Anglo-American common law. The traditional rejection of suicide in Anglo-American culture has been grounded in the common law's solicitousness toward vulnerable persons—including older persons, and persons who are mentally incompetent—through the criminal law. . . .

Suicide, a felony at common law, was regarded as "self-murder." Cyril Means, among others, has concluded upon examination of its history at common law that suicide is not protected as a constitutional right: "Throughout its long history, the common law has always set its face against suicide. . . ." The difficulty of penalizing the successful perpetrator was at the foundation of American law's failure to penalize suicide. However, even where the states failed to penalize suicide, many states penalized those who assisted suicide.

Wrong Meaning

Did emergence of the right to privacy have any bearing on suicide? What is today called the right to privacy had its early development in the Brandeis-Warren *Harvard Law Review* article of 1890. In its original formulation, the Brandeis-Warren right to privacy was a right to informational family privacy. Viewed in the context of its relationship to the laws of homicide and suicide, the right to privacy did not encompass a right to suicide or to be free from interventions to prevent suicide.

The common law has protected a right to refuse medical treatment. The so-called right to die is an unfortunate and inaccurate misnomer of very recent origin. As a phrase in increasingly common use, however, it reflects the abandonment of the traditional right to refuse medical treatment. That right of refusal connoted the right—not to seek death—but to avoid the imposition of a medical treatment that is simultaneously burdensome or painful and ineffective in averting imminent and inevitable death from a terminal illness. To transmute a right to refuse medical treatment into a "right to die," however, switches the focus from the burden of nonbeneficial medical treatment to the desire for death itself. . . .

The common law's rejection of suicide on any grounds demonstrates that the common law has not protected the unfettered autonomy that serves as the rationale for the recent campaign for legalized suicide. The common law's solicitous protection of vulnerable patients reveals its protection for the sanctity of human life at all stages and its respect for the dignity of human life without regard to physical condition. And its regulation of guardians reflects the law's recognition that vulnerable patients need to be protected from the emotional, financial, or psychological burdens that often affect the persons to whose care they have seen entrusted.

If one were to look strictly at the state statutes presently on the books, it would not seem that the prospects for the legalization of assisted suicide in the near future are very good. At least twenty-six states by statute expressly prohibit the assistance of suicide. Moreover, living will statutes have been enacted in at least forty states, including Washington, D.C., but the statutes in no less than ten states, including Washington, D.C., expressly repudiate suicide and euthanasia, albeit with no penalties. No states expressly legalize suicide through either legislation or constitution.

Suicide Contradicts Life

If a man destroys his body, and so his life, he does it by the use of his will, which is itself destroyed in the process. But to use the power of a free will for its own destruction is self-contradictory. If freedom is the condition of life it cannot be employed to abolish life and so to destroy and abolish itself. To use life for its own destruction, to use life for producing lifelessness, is self-contradictory. . . . Man cannot rightly have any power of disposal in regard to himself and his life.

Immanuel Kant in *Suicide: Right or Wrong?*, 1990.

This survey of legislation may be misleading, however. The introduction of assisted suicide into American law will more likely come through current judicial trends in the nontreatment of incompetent patients than through explicit legislative acceptance. There is an evident and increasing tension in judicial decisions signaling efforts to transmute the right to refuse medical treatment into the "right to die.". . .

By both depreciating society's compelling interest in the sanctity of human life and in adopting substituted judgment, recent court decisions have laid the groundwork for the ultimate approval of suicide and assisted suicide.

Right to Control

Beyond recent case law, there have been calls for the legalization of "rational suicide" through legislation. It is claimed that a right to suicide is protected under the liberty clauses of the fifth and fourteenth amendments to the Constitution. Derek Humphry, for example, has claimed that the case for legalized euthanasia and suicide stems from the privacy doctrine of *Roe v. Wade*. Short of constitutional protection, a right to "rational suicide" has been proposed as good public policy based on

26

principles of autonomy and self-determination—the right to control one's body, destiny, and health care.

"Rational suicide" has as many different definitions as there are advocates. A "rational suicide" may be one undertaken by a patient "beyond all help and not merely suffering from a treatable depression of the sort common in people with terminal illnesses," or "[i]f there is no treatable component to the depression and the patient's pain or suffering is refractory to treatment, then the wish for suicide may be rational."

Sanctity of Human Life

Those who currently propose assisted suicide contend that life is only one among a number of goods, including individual autonomy, human dignity, intellectual capability, physical fitness, and other aspects that contribute to personal well-being. Life as a relative good must be compared with other goods, and suicide may become a "rational" choice if life has become "intolerable."

A second, but related, principle that is used to justify suicide is personal autonomy. The push for "patient autonomy" in medical ethics over the past twenty years has spurred the drive for euthanasia and suicide. Suicide is seen as a wholly individual act, a self-directed act, a "victimless crime." Whereas the traditional understanding has been that society has a compelling interest in preserving human life and preventing suicide, proponents of suicide contend that society has no legitimate interest in interfering in an act as personal as "rational" suicide.

The principle of the sanctity of human life, on the other hand, demands that human beings must always be treated as an end in themselves and should never be treated as a means to an end. The sanctity of human life is a paramount value; it is the denial of the sanctity of human life, rather than the denial of individual autonomy by prohibiting suicide, that violates human dignity. Human dignity is violated by failing to treat human beings as ends in themselves, by considering their physical or mental conditions as the measure of the value of their lives. In contrast, human dignity is protected by preserving a person's life, confirming the value of that person's life, and promoting that person's well-being, without regard to the physical or mental condition of the person.

Privacy Issue

Privacy is clearly a right that the American people cherish and enjoy. But the invocation of privacy or autonomy nearly always begs the question—privacy to do what? Autonomy to do what? More than one hundred years ago, during the Lincoln-Douglas Senate debates of 1858, Abraham Lincoln pointed out the boundaries of autonomy. Lincoln acknowledged that there were differences of opinion on the slavery question, but, to his mind, the "difference of opinion, reduced to its lowest terms, is no other than the difference between the men who think slavery a wrong and those who do not think it wrong." Lincoln pointed out that it was logically impossible for Douglas to say both that slavery was wrong and that the people had a right to have slaves:

> When Judge Douglas says that whoever or whatever community wants slaves, they have a right to have them, he is perfectly logical if there is nothing wrong in the institution; but if you admit that it is wrong, he cannot logically say that any body has a right to do wrong.

There is no "right" to do what is intrinsically wrong, and Anglo-American law and culture have always held suicide to be intrinsically wrong. It must be remembered that the Declaration of Independence refers to the right to life as an "unalienable" right and, thus, a right that cannot be waived or forfeited.

The location of an action alone does not shield the act from moral or legal scrutiny. Private actions are not shielded from scrutiny merely because the acts are committed in the home or between family members. The publicized outcry in recent years over child abuse and spousal abuse makes it clear that the American public understands this, at least in some cases. . . .

Depression as Cause

The notion of "rational suicide" is also belied by studies that have concluded that the desire for death, even among terminal patients, is the result of a preexisting mental illness and not a product of sober, rational calculation. A general examination of recent suicides reveals that the typical suicide was motivated not by sober rational reasons, but by depression, a state of mind that is present in many older persons. Among the factors that motivate suicide in people of all ages are the same factors that result in depression generally—loss of a job through forced retirement, rapid urbanization and technological change, alcoholism, a universal fear of dependence and frailty, and illness. According to Daniel Plotkin, a geriatric psychiatrist at the University of California at Los Angeles, most suicides among older persons are caused not by terminal illness but by depression. Similarly, adolescent suicide is often a response to depression and feelings of hopelessness.

The call for legalized suicide based on autonomy, then, is not what it seems. The evidence suggests that "patient autonomy" is not truly autonomous. This is most clearly seen in the courts' adoption in recent years of the doctrine of substituted judgment, the "cruel charade," in Justice Joseph R. Nolan's words. Even if we accept this autonomy at face value, it reflects exactly the desire for self-destruction that lies at the basis of the common law's long-held rejection of suicide and its corresponding devotion to the principle of the sanctity of human life. It is an autonomy that calls for the compassionate care and devotion of the physician who is committed to the welfare of his patient, not the destruction of the patient, either self-induced or assisted.

Legal and Medical Consequences

A right to assisted suicide may be a logical development of the current push for the withdrawal of assisted feeding from severely disabled patients. Judicial authorization of the withdrawal of life-sustaining food and fluids from patients who are not terminally ill nor imminently dying will inevitably create pressure in both law and medical practice to journey down the slippery slope toward use of lethal injections to hasten the death of a patient in a more "humane" manner. . . .

A Nation Drunk on Rights

The right to die sounds as all-American as the class action suit. It partakes of the flavor of individual autonomy. Are we not each the captain of our own ship? No one can tell you what you can or cannot do with your own body. Whose life is it anyway?

We're a nation drunk on rights, and always willing to have just one more for the road. . . . Suicides are famous for two things. The first is despair. The second is changing their minds. Dr. Walter D. Charen, a Hartford psychiatrist, has written, "even despairing individuals in deep depression are ambivalent about suicide. They waver time and again between life and death.". . .

What suicide proponents don't understand is that no individual is completely independent. We need each other—all the more so when we are sick or dying. Propounding suicide or euthanasia as the answer to suffering—when care and comfort are what's missing—is a ghastly, nightmarish solution, morally corrupt at the core.

Mona Charen, *Conservative Chronicle*, October 23, 1991.

The recent article by Sidney Wanzer and others in the *New England Journal of Medicine* on "The Physician's Responsibility Toward Hopelessly Ill Patients" remarkably endorses actions traditionally considered irresponsible. The authors seem to concede that "rational suicide" is really born of distress, stating that "only the rare patient should be so distressed that he or she desires to commit suicide." Ten of the twelve authors conclude that it *is* justifiable for the physician to assist suicide when "(1) [t]he doctor, the nurse, the family and the patient . . . have done everything possible to relieve the distress occasioned by a terminal illness, (2) and yet the patient perceives his or her situation as *intolerable* and seeks assistance. . . ." They conclude that "[t]he

29

physician . . . must determine first that the patient is indeed beyond all help and not merely suffering from a treatable depression of the sort common in people with terminal illnesses." And, "[i]f there is no treatable component to the depression and the patient's pain or suffering is refractory to treatment, then the wish for suicide may be rational." Is the author's message here a version of "If you can't beat 'em, join 'em"? If you can't cure the patient's desires, join him in fulfilling his desires? "Rational suicide,". . . has no secure semantic fence around it to prevent abuse. A 1986 note on "Criminal Liability for Assisting Suicide" in the *Columbia University Law Review* proposed a Model Suicide Assistance Statute that could allow assisted suicide for any "competent adult who was suffering from *permanent physical incapacitation*"—whatever that means. The inability to regulate "rational suicide" will quickly result in an unfettered "right" that is exercised by anyone, for "rational" or irrational motives.

"The sense of a personal self-sacrifice is part of the concept of rational, balance sheet suicide."

Suicide Can Be a Rational Choice

Alan W. Johnson

In the following viewpoint, Alan W. Johnson contends that certain people, especially the terminally ill, can make a rational decision to commit suicide. He states that legal restrictions that prevent the terminally ill from committing suicide deny them their civil rights and cause the ill to endure further pain. He concludes that it is possible to make a rational decision to commit suicide because individuals can evaluate the quality of their lives and determine that death would be better than life. Johnson has been on the national board of The Hemlock Society and is presently the head of The Hemlock Society in Palm Springs, California.

As you read, consider the following questions:

1. How does Johnson contrast the deaths of his mother and stepmother?
2. What is the author's definition of rational suicide?
3. Why does Johnson believe that a person can make a rational decision to commit suicide?

I do not choose to die in diapers!" Those were her exact words.

I was singularly fortunate to have had not one but two remarkable mothers. My natural mother was a humanitarian, social democrat, and philanthropist, founder of the now 77 year old Francis W. Parker School, San Diego, one of the west's leading college preparatory institutions. She had a heart as big as the whole outdoors, and she thought with it. Having lived for others, at ninety-one she drifted away after a 15 month decline at home, in diapers.

Choice of Death

But it was my stepmother who uttered the injunctive words above. She had been in a volunteer ambulance unit in World War I, right behind the trenches in Belgium. Losing her first husband, a journalist, to spinal meningitis in 1923, she drew on her war experience to become a Red Cross professional at the U.S. Naval Hospital, San Diego. When World War II exploded, she was placed in charge of all Red Cross operations at the Naval Training Station, with thirty-seven social workers under her direction. She was a person of great dignity and grace. When at age eighty-three she began a three year slide, suffering from emphysema and a variety of other complications, she would have none of it. "Alan," she would say, "you know what I have been. This isn't 'living' any more! Can't you get me a gun or a pill? I want to get out of here. I've had two wonderful husbands and a good career, but now my life is finished. I want to end it!" Having to be put in diapers was just a final indignity which she did not want to bear.

I learned a great deal about dying from those two wonderful women, one going relatively quickly, with quiet resignation until she slipped away; the other feistily wanting still to exercise her powers of analysis and decision, honed over those years of serving the needs of others. The first died at peace. The second went through the dying process in rebellion, suffering both physical and psychological agony. Not her style, she deserved better!

Basic Human Right

What is the issue here? Gloria Steinem's lead paragraph of an article, "A Basic Human Right," highlights it. "The most crucial question of democracy, feminism, and simple self-respect is not: *What* gets decided? That comes second. The first question is: *Who* decides?" Though she was writing about women's reproductive rights, the same principle applies to the right to decide about dying. The right to choose when, where, and how to die is as fundamental as any, certainly as much so as the abortion question. Think of it as a sort of final civil right! And is it also a

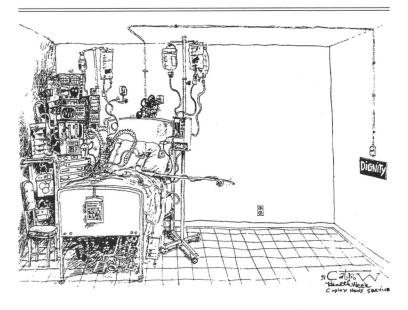

Dave Catrow/Copley News Service. Reprinted with permission.

women's issue? You'd better believe it!

Decisions about dying are of particular importance to older women. Why? Because it is generally they who are left. First, many have to cope with the exigencies of their husbands' dying. Often they are ill prepared to do so because their husbands have not executed a Living Will or, more importantly, have not completed a well-conceived Durable Power of Attorney for Health Care. Under great emotional tension and with feelings of ambivalence, they frequently must deal with doctors and hospitals about treatments which their husbands shall or shall not receive. Will they prolong their lives beneficially, or will they simply prolong suffering while dying? This is at a time when competency of the husbands to make decisions is already gone or is impaired because of pain and medication. Then, in over 80% of marriages, the husbands predecease their wives, leaving them to cope with adjusting to a new phase of life. What happens to them?

According to an earlier report from the American Medical Association, there are at any given time in this country approximately 10,000 persons, mostly women, in nursing homes living out a meager remainder of their lives. It has been documented that many receive substandard care. They are simply being warehoused. A significant number are nearly or fully comatose or, if not, being sedated so that they are easier to manage. For many, life no longer has any real meaning. Its burdens exceed its benefits. As many reach the terminal stage, often suffering the ravages of painful and debilitating diseases, they express their wish to die sooner rather than later. Only in the Netherlands can this now be accomplished humanely through the assistance of physicians, acting under a set of guidelines devised by the Dutch Medical Society and promulgated by the High Court of the Netherlands.

Changing the Law

If a person in this country is competent and, though terminal, still able to function, she/he may opt for voluntary euthanasia, i.e., rational suicide. Using published information available from the National Hemlock Society, this may be carefully planned and carried out, provided the means can be secured. A quick, gentle death by overdose is a preference of many, but some equally effective ways are available. There is no longer any law against suicide in modern, civilized countries. Physician aid in dying is safer for the patient and even now sometimes covertly agreed upon between patient and doctor and carried out. The doctor does incur a degree of risk, for to assist in a suicide is a felony in nearly every U.S. jurisdiction. To enable terminally ill people to exercise their choice to die sooner than later, and to do so under safe and carefully controlled conditions, the National Hemlock Society believes that the law should be changed to provide for physician assistance in dying. So does another organization, on whose board I sit, Americans Against Human Suffering. . . .

The Courts

Refer back to Steinem's dictum; "The first question is: *Who* decides?" Is this a matter for individual decision? Let's look at who is deciding now. Decisions about who shall decide are, with increasing frequency, made in the courts. . . .

With surprising frequency, trial courts have supported decisions of doctors and hospitals over the wishes of patients and their surrogates. It has been the appellate courts which time after time have overruled, granting relief, placing the decision-making responsibility back in the hands of individuals and their surrogates. In a penetrating analysis of the reasonings in many of these cases, however, one of the country's leading ethicists, Prof. Joseph Fletcher, argues that the courts have been coming up with the right findings but often for reasons which cannot stand the tests of pure logic. They are caught up, he says, in semantic misinterpretations of terms such as "euthanasia," "passive," or "active," or are as subject as many to the weight of custom, tradition, and taboos, skirting real issues when articulating decisions which they feel are in the interests of justice for the welfare of patients. . . .

The law in virtually every U.S. jurisdiction . . . makes it a felony to assist another person to commit suicide. Despite this law, numbers of "mercy killings" have been rising dramatically. What does this law do to your freedom of choice? For many who come to the point of not wanting to linger, they are no longer able to try to provide themselves with the means of achieving a quiet, pain-free, dignified death. If they ask a friend or a doctor for help in dying, they are asking them to place themselves in jeopardy under this law. Some will do it, as a matter of compassion, but it is a terrible risk. It also raises the question: is suicide morally right or wrong, and under what circumstances? Beyond that, what do we mean by suicide? . . .

What Is Suicide?

Is the soldier who throws himself on a grenade to prevent injury or death of his comrades in battle committing suicide? Or take the case of the passenger in the airplane taking off from National Airport, Washington, which, icing up, crashed into the Potomac. That passenger swam to assist five others to safety, only to lose his own life. Would you call that suicide or a rational act of self-sacrifice? Suppose that a friend of yours becomes terminally ill, then hears from a trusted doctor a prognosis that the disease is ultimately incurable and that even to try to ameliorate the condition will involve considerable suffering and pain. What if the friend decides that to go sooner rather than later is a wholly rational approach to the problem, easier on patient and family and friends? Would that be a right or wrong decision? By whose standards? Should the patient have the right to make that choice?

Rational Suicide

Doris Portwood describes "balance sheet" suicide: that it is "possible for a perfectly sane person, thinking logically, to set off the unacceptable or intolerable aspects of his or her life against the chances for betterment and find the result weighted on the side of death." Cases are known of persons facing up to the inevitability of terminal illness who maintain, "I'd rather conserve my estate for my heirs and beneficiaries than spend a lot of money on medical procedures which can only prove useless in the end." That too, in the sense of a personal self-sacrifice, is part of the concept of rational, balance sheet suicide.

Most certainly, the emotional difficulties which lead persons, many of them young, to contemplate suicide—but for all the wrong reasons—should be afforded treatment through counseling, providing the understanding and support needed to reorient their lives in positive directions. The second General Principle of the National Hemlock Society reads: "HEMLOCK does not encourage suicide for any primary emotional, traumatic, or financial reasons in the absence of terminal illness. It approves of the work of those involved in suicide prevention." But it also supports "the option of [rational suicide] for the terminally ill." Terminally ill persons should have the freedom so to choose. Yet many terminally ill, thoughtfully analytical enough to acknowledge the certainty that such a day will come and wishing to plan ahead for the eventualities, are caught in the bind of often not being able to exercise their choice effectively.

A Rational Decision

In order for an action to be deemed rational, it must involve effective deliberation and a realistic assessment of possibilities. This is especially true for the action of self-annihilation: life is precious, and should not be given up lightly. But there are demonstrable cases of rational suicides, such as the example of the noted Freudian scholar Bruno Bettelheim, who took his own life after determining that its quality had so seriously deteriorated that he no longer wished to go on living. In this, he was emulating Freud himself, who in his final hours told his doctor, Max Schur: "My dear Schur, you remember our 'contract' not to leave me in the lurch when the time has come. Now it is nothing but torture and makes no sense." Schur, a longtime friend of Freud's, thereupon gave him a large dose of morphine, which brought about a coma from which Freud did not awake.

Tim Madigan, *Free Inquiry*, Fall 1990.

They may be physically or economically unable to secure the desired means of self-deliverance. They may be afraid that they would botch the job. They may hesitate to involve any friend in helping them. They may be already in a hospital or nursing home, a setting in which it is almost impossible to give effect to their desires. It is this quandary which Americans Against Human Suffering is trying to overcome through proposing to make a small but significant change in the law to provide a new option for the terminally ill, a new freedom for choice. . . .

If passed into law, [the] benefits become available to any competent adult to use if wished. It is of most use to clear headed persons who recognize dying and death as simply the last act of life, inevitable, and therefore to be considered in advance and dealt with through the same processes of rational analysis and decision making as any other problem faced in life. . . .

Some say that there has never been a law created which could not be abused. Perhaps so, but by placing the right to choose squarely in the hands of an individual citizen and the sole right to help a terminally ill person to die in the hands of a physician who must exercise that right according to the stated desires of the patient and requirements of the law, abuses certainly ought to be minimal. Look at it another way: who now is being abused and to what extent? Isn't it those thousands and thousands of terminally ill persons, mostly elderly women, who, for lack of a law like this, must suffer on interminably when they want to die sooner, when life no longer serves a beneficial purpose and there's no fun anymore? The real abusers are those persons who wish to inflict their own particular dogmatic standards upon all the rest of us and who thus will rail against enactment of a law like this. It is incomprehensible that they can be so pro-suffering. This law will not force them to do one single thing. It may offend their particular sensibilities, but in no way will it do them any material or personal harm.

Perhaps Jefferson's words in the Declaration of Independence are the most apt when considering this proposal: "Life, Liberty, and the Pursuit of Happiness." What is Life but a collection of feeling and thinking individuals, each respected as unique in a democratic society? What is Liberty more than the privilege of each one of us to exercise freedom of choice and action, providing that it is exercised responsibly so as not to harm others or impinge upon their own rights? What is Happiness other than to do the best we can for ourselves and others while alive so that we can die happily, with pride, with respect, and with dignity?

"We must not fall for the calm and matter-of-fact talk of 'rational suicide.' "

Suicide Can Never Be a Rational Choice

Leon R. Kass

Leon R. Kass, a trained physician and biochemist at the University of Chicago, is an outspoken critic of the right-to-die movement. In the following viewpoint, he argues that there is no such thing as rational suicide. He believes that the motivation for suicide comes from an emotional rather than a rational state. Kass contends the term rational suicide is used by those who do not want to take responsibility for the ill and depressed.

As you read, consider the following questions:

1. Why does Kass use Derek Humphry's book to warn about the danger of rational suicide?
2. According to the author, how has medical technology affected death?
3. Why does Kass believe suicide is an emotional rather than a rational choice?

Excerpted from Leon R. Kass, "Suicide Made Easy: The Evil of Rational Suicide." Reprinted from *Commentary*, December 1991, by permission. All rights reserved. (Subheadings and inserted quotations added by Greenhaven editors.)

Americans have always been a handy people. If know-how were virtue, we would be a nation of saints. Unfortunately, certain old-fashioned taboos—brought to you by the people who know the difference between virtue and dexterity—have prevented Americans from gaining the ultimate know-how, the know-how to die. Until now. Riding atop the best-seller lists, outdistancing other manuals of self-help like *The Seven Habits of Highly Effective People*, *The T-Factor Fat Gram Counter*, and *Wealth Without Risk*, is Derek Humphry's latest book, *Final Exit*, subtitled "The Practicalities of Self-Deliverance and Assisted Suicide for the Dying." Know-how in spades.

What can one say about this new "book"? In one word: evil. I did not want to read it, I do not want you to read it. It should never have been written, and it does not deserve to be dignified with a review, let alone an article. Yet it stares out at us from nearly every bookstore window, beckoning us to learn how to achieve the final solution—for ourselves or for those we (allegedly) love so much that we will help them kill themselves. Says the Lord High Executioner, Derek Humphry, prophet of Hemlock: I have set before thee life and death: therefore choose death. "Courageous," bleat the media; "Timely." "Rational." "Humane." Is there no one who will call evil by its proper name?

This is not the usual and notorious evil of malicious intent or violent manner; this is humanitarian evil, evil with a smile: well-meaning, gentle, and rational, especially rational. For this reason it is both harder to recognize as evil and harder to combat. Yet, also for this reason, it deserves our most vigilant attention, for it is an exquisite model of modern rationalism gone wrong, while looking oh so right. . . .

Plausible Verdict

If suicide (and its assistance) is to be justified by a right to choose the time and manner of one's death, if the right of life, liberty, and the pursuit of happiness or the so-called right of privacy encompasses also a "right to die," then (as Humphry argues) the whole matter is "too personal" and subjective; and the case for suicide need not rest on *any* objective or demonstrable criteria—such as certifiable terminal illness or truly intractable pain. For who is to say what makes life "unbearable," or death "electable," for another person? The autonomy argument kicks out all criteria for evaluating the choice, save that it be uncoerced.

Of course no one, not even Humphry, wants to leave it at that. Instead, reasons are given to justify choosing death: too much pain, loss of dignity, lack of self-command, poor quality of life. These are supposed to add up to a plausible verdict: life is no longer worth living. Such "useless" or "degrading" or "dehumanized" lives now plead for active, "merciful" termination. . . .

Once suicide and assisting suicide are okay, for reasons of "mercy," then delivering the dehumanized is okay, whether chosen or not. Humphry and his crowd are well aware of the slippery slope. Yet pretending to want only a partial slide, they have both embraced the principle and started us on a decline that will take us all the way—to eliminating everyone deemed unfit.

Steve Benson. Reprinted by permission: Tribune Media Services.

This is already happening in Holland. . . .

The newly released report of the government's Committee to Investigate the Practice of Euthanasia in Holland contains the most extensive and most reliable information to date on euthanasia in the Netherlands. Its reassuring conclusions are, to say the least, at great variance with the wealth of disturbing data it provides. Here are just a few of the findings: 25,300 cases of euthanasia (active and passive) occur in the Netherlands every year, 19.4 percent of all deaths in the country. These include 1,000 cases of *direct active involuntary* euthanasia. In addition, there are 8,100 cases in which morphine was overdosed with the intention to terminate life, 61 percent of the time without the patient's knowledge or consent. And there are another 8,750 cases in which life-preserving treatment was stopped or withheld without consent of the patient and with the intention to shorten life. "Low quality of life," "no prospect of improvement," and "the family could not take it anymore" were among the most frequently cited reasons to terminate patients' lives without their consent. In 45 percent of cases in which the lives of hospital patients were actively terminated without their consent, this was done without the knowledge of the families. Are you duly reassured?

The Way of Madness

Let me not be misunderstood. Dying in our technological age, even in humanitarian institutions, often comes attended by horrors unknown to our ancestors, often as an unintentional consequence of medical success in the battle against death. Medicine or no medicine, mortality remains our lot. Yet our secular and utopian culture does not prepare us well to face this truth and its consequences. Both painful personal experience and serious study for over two decades have taught me to appreciate deeply the anguish and fear of patients and families in the myriad matters surrounding decay and death; I know and feel the horror of the way many of us now end our lives. There are many, many circumstances—too numerous, too particular, too nuanced to lay out in advance—that call for the cessation of medical intervention, even if death comes as a result. There is rarely a good reason for withholding proper doses of pain medication, even if providing effective analgesia runs an increased risk of earlier death. And there is much more that we can do—most of it a matter of human relations, not of technological devices—to support the morale and dignity of people faced with incurable or fatal illness. But to cross the line and accept active euthanasia, mercy killing, "aid-in-dying," death from doctor's healing hand, "dignified autoeuthanasia," and "self-deliverance"—that way lies madness.

At the very least, we must now open our eyes to the situation before us. We must not allow ourselves to be gulled by euphemisms and by falsely calming images like "final exit." We must not accept Humphry's shallow notion that "dignity" can be delivered by a hypodermic needle filled with lethal medicine. We must not forget the cost-containers and the eugenicists who stand ready in the wings to exploit the "choice" for death, to make sure that the burdensome and incurable take advantage of the deadly option. And above all, we must not fall for the calm and matter-of-fact talk of "rational suicide."

Calmness and coolness are, by themselves, no proof of rationality. Neither is deliberate planning, or the stockpiling of "magic pills." All human conduct is motivated—by desire or fear or some other appetite or emotion; thought alone moves nothing. However much Humphry talks of rationality—"It was not done out of cowardice or escapism but from long-held rational beliefs"; "Very, very few physicians will prescribe a lethal dose for a fit person. The stigma of being associated with a possible emotional suicide (as distinct from a rational suicide) is too risky"; etc.—the truth is that passions, sentiments, desires drive our every action. In the case of those explicitly addressed by this book, the dominant motives—the true movers of the soul—will be fear, resignation, and despair, or, in other words, the desire to escape. It is surely not pure reason that finds life unbearable.

One Cannot Choose Death

The wish "I want to die" might be a confused statement masking any number of unarticulated wishes: "I want to punish you, and you, and you"; "I want to punish the loathsome creature that appears to be myself"; "I want to be taken up by my Creator, and returned to the bliss of my first home"; "I want to alter my life because it is so disappointing, or painful, or boring"; "I want to silence the voices that are always shouting instructions"; "I want—I know not what." Rationally one cannot "choose" Death because Death is an unknown experience, and perhaps it isn't even an "experience"—perhaps it is simply nothing; and one cannot imagine nothing.

Joyce Carol Oates in *Suicide: Right or Wrong?*, 1990.

Let's get serious about "rationality" and reason. Do we know what we are talking about when we claim that someone can *rationally* choose nonbeing or nothingness? How can poor reason even contemplate nothingness, much less accurately calculate its merits as compared with continued existence? What we have in so-called rational suicide is a mere rationality of means, rationality of technique, but utter *non*-rationality regarding the end and its putative goodness. An act of "rational suicide" may be psychologically understandable and (even, in some cases) morally pardonable, but it is utterly *un*reasonable.

Humphry and others contend that it is religious dogma alone, not human reason, which regards suicide as unethical. But this is patent nonsense. Immanuel Kant, whose claim to rationality is second to none, regarded the will to suicide as inherently self-contradictory, and thus, precisely, irrational:

It seems absurd that a man can injure himself (*volenti non fit injuria* [Injury cannot happen to one who is willing]). The Stoic therefore considered it a prerogative of his personality as a wise man to walk out of this life with an undisturbed mind whenever he liked (as out of a smoke-filled room), not because he was afflicted by actual or anticipated ills, but simply because he could make use of nothing more in this life. And yet this very courage, this strength of mind—of not fearing death and of knowing of something which man can prize more

42

highly than his life—ought to have been an ever so much greater motive for him not to destroy himself, a being having such authoritative superiority over the strongest sensible incentives; consequently, it ought to have been a motive for him not to deprive himself of life.

Man cannot deprive himself of his personhood so long as one speaks of duties, thus so long as he lives. That man ought to have the authorization to withdraw himself from all obligation, i.e., to be free to act as if no authorization at all were required for this withdrawal, involves a contradiction. To destroy the subject of morality in his own person is tantamount to obliterating from the world, as far as he can, the very existence of morality itself; but morality is, nevertheless, an end in itself. Accordingly, to dispose of oneself as a mere means to some end of one's own liking is to degrade the humanity in one's person (*homo noumenon*), which, after all, was entrusted to man (*homo phaenomenon*) to preserve.

So-called "rational suicide" is finally a sophism. Those who preach it and abet it are teachers of evil.

Defending Human Decency

Modern rationalism, whose leading branch is modern natural science and whose purest fruit is medical technology, has certainly made human life less poor, brutish, and short. Yet because, being morally neutral, it knows only the means, never the end, it has left us lost at sea without a compass. Worst of all, blinded by pride in our technique, we do not even suspect that we are lost, that we have become, as Churchill put it, "the sport and presently the victim of tides and currents, whirlpools and tornadoes amid which [we are] far more helpless than [we have] been for a long time." We do not yet understand that the project for the mastery of nature and the conquest of death leads only to dehumanization; that any attempt to gain the tree of life by means of the tree of knowledge leads inevitably also to the hemlock; and that the utter rationalization of life under the banner of the will tragically produces a world in which we all get to become senile and in which our loved ones get to do us in.

The taboos against homicide, suicide, and euthanasia—like those against incest, adultery, and fornication, central insights of the receding wisdom from a more sensible age—are today weak and increasingly defenseless against the rising tide of gentle dehumanization. Yet they are all that stands between us and the flood. Everyone who cares truly for human dignity and decency—that is, everyone who would be truly rational—must now come to their defense, before it is too late.

The Ability to Empathize

Whether an individual has a right to commit suicide is a subject of debate. Proponents of suicide for the terminally ill see it as an expression of individual choice. For them, suicide is a comforting option that frees the terminally ill from being stuck in a hospital room facing unbearable pain and unnecessary suffering. They believe suicide can be a rational decision and argue that laws should be passed to respect this decision.

In contrast, opponents contend that there is no such thing as the right to commit suicide. Suicide is an emotional, not a rational decision, these critics maintain. They contend that suicidal patients suffer from depression, which should be treated. In addition, they argue that medicine can effectively control the pain and suffering of the dying. For opponents, suicide is not an option to be considered, even for the terminally ill.

There are many terminally ill people who face the dilemma of whether to commit suicide or to continue living. Consider the following personal account, which is the true story of a mother who asks her daughter to help her commit suicide. As you read, try to empathize with the mother and daughter. The ability to empathize, to see a situation from another person's vantage point, is an important skill. When we empathize, we put ourselves in someone else's position. This helps us to look at a problem in a way that we perhaps have not considered before. The ability to understand an opponent's viewpoint is a difficult skill, one that is needed for a highly emotional and controversial subject like suicide.

Barbara's Story

It is time for me to tell my mother's story. After watching her mind deteriorate slowly over five years, and after ten months of prayerful discernment and planning, my mother quietly and with great dignity and grace ended her life. She had my support and the help of a compassionate physician who prescribed sleeping pills for her. For over 40 years my mother was my closest confidant, guide and friend. To help her die was the only thing she ever asked of me. I sought guidance in prayer and from Christian friends before agreeing to help her.

She had worked as a volunteer at the local geriatric center and was intimately aware of end-stage Alzheimer's disease. She told me that every time she walked out of the center she prayed that it would not happen to her. But she realized that she probably had it even then. The neurologist who diagnosed her told her "there is no treatment," and sent her to a psychiatrist because her mother had taken her own life after her children had grown up and left home. This had devastated my mother and she never got over the shock. She swore that she would never do it to me. But this was different, she said. And it was.

She endured 12 years of widowhood alone, maintaining staunchly that she would never live with her children. We had bought a big house so that there would be plenty of room for her, and my husband repeatedly invited her to move in with us. But her pride and her close connection to many friends prevented her from coming until the Alzheimer's had so exhausted her that she could no longer live alone and the disease was interfering with her relationships.

By the time she moved in, six months before she died, she was unable to pursue any of her interests. Getting up was a chore. She could no longer read because she didn't know what the words meant; she forgot words and was embarrassed to speak at length. She could no longer recognize the denominations of money; on several occasions she could not remember my father's name. She no longer wanted to shower, woke up confused and became incontinent at night, and began to hallucinate during the day. She developed gout and angina, in addition to the arthritis and glaucoma which were chronic but under control. Her hearing was also impaired, and this increased her difficulty in communicating.

A Final Blessing

But her time with us and our twin sons was delightful. We went to the opera and concerts and out to dinner. She shared their 21st birthday celebration, and was able to give them her car as a birthday gift. All the while she and we were planning how she could end her life without posing legal dangers to the doctor or to me and yet without dying alone or among strangers. She came up with the plan to visit her sister and rent a hotel room.

She said good-by to the children as they left for college. They had no idea what was about to happen. She was very strong. My husband and I dropped her off and she said good-by to us quickly. She looked beautiful. After the last dinner on the night before I was to "pick her up," she emptied the powder from the pills into her favorite food to disguise the taste.

When I arrived the next morning she was peacefully curled up in bed, having died painlessly and without fuss in her sleep. Her doctor came immediately and pronounced her dead and agreed to write on the death certificate that she died of a massive stroke. Her friends and family took it as a blessing, even a reward from God for the pure and blameless life she had lived. I only wish I could tell them how truly valiant and courageous she really was.

Consider the following questions:
1. What would you do if you were in the situation presented in the story? Why?
2. Do you think someone can make a rational choice to die? Why?
3. If someone close to you were suffering and near death, what type of arguments would you use in order to defend his or her right to die?
4. If someone close to you were dying in pain and wanted to commit suicide, what arguments would you use to convince him or her to live?
5. How do you think Leon R. Kass, the author of viewpoint 4 in this chapter, would respond to the situation presented in the story?

Periodical Bibliography

The following articles have been selected to supplement the diverse views presented in this chapter.

Katherine Ames, Larry Wilson, Daniel Glick, and Patricia King	"Last Rights," *Newsweek*, August 26, 1991.
Marcia Angell	"The Right to Die in Dignity," *Newsweek*, July 23, 1990.
Bonnie Angelo	"Assigning the Blame for a Young Man's Suicide," *Time*, November 18, 1991.
Stephen Chapman	"When Life Is Worse Than Death, Who Chooses?" *Conservative Chronicle*, April 4, 1990. Available from PO Box 11297, Des Moines, IA 50340-1297.
Yeates Conwell and Eric D. Caine	"Rational Suicide and the Right to Die," *The New England Journal of Medicine*, October 10, 1991. Available from PO Box 803, Waltham, MA 02254-0803.
Derek Humphry	"The Right to Choose to Die," *American Atheist*, June 1990.
Issues	"Janet Adkins' Suicide: Reexamining the Spectrum of Issues It Has Raised," July/August 1990. Available from managing editor, 477 N. Lindbergh Blvd., St. Louis, MO 63141.
Maria McFadden	"Suicide—The Next Choice," *Human Life Review*, Winter 1991. Available from The Human Life Foundation, Inc., Editorial Office, Room 840, 150 E. 35th St., New York, NY 10016.
Charles E. Rice	"Killing with Kindness," *The New American*, February 10, 1992. Available from PO Box 8040, Appleton, WI 54913.
Peter Steinfels	"At Crossroads, U.S. Ponders Ethics of Helping Others Die," *The New York Times*, October 28, 1991.
Lilian Stevens	"For an Ill Widow, 83, Suicide Is Welcome," *The New York Times*, August 4, 1989.
James M. Wall	"In the Face of Death: Rights, Choices, Beliefs," *The Christian Century*, August 21-28, 1991.
Susan M. Wolf	"Final Exit: The End of Argument," *Hastings Center Report*, January/February 1992.

Should Physicians Assist Terminally Ill Patients in Suicide?

Chapter Preface

Janet Adkins was a wife, mother, teacher, musician, and lover of the outdoors who was diagnosed with Alzheimer's disease. To spare her family and herself what she called "the agony of this terrible disease," she contacted Dr. Jack Kevorkian to assist her in committing suicide. After months of discussion with Adkins and her family by phone, Kevorkian made an appointment to see her on Monday, June 4, 1990. They met in Kevorkian's rusty old van at Groveland Park in north Oakland County, Michigan. Once Adkins was comfortably situated on the built-in bed, Kevorkian attached a device with an intravenous solution to her right arm and electrocardiograph electrodes to her ankles and wrists. She pressed a switch and released the solution that killed her in six minutes.

When Kevorkian's involvement in Adkin's death became public, the reactions ranged from praise to condemnation. A November 3, 1991, poll taken by the *Boston Globe* and the Harvard School of Public Health revealed that 64 percent of Americans favored physician-assisted suicide. Yet in that same month, the citizens of Washington state voted down legislation that would have permitted physicians to assist their patients in suicide. These seemingly contradictory responses underscore that the issue of assisted suicide is emotionally charged and complicated.

Opponents view the topic from a variety of perspectives. From an ethical standpoint, the Hippocratic oath is regarded as the standard ethic for doctors. The oath states that physicians should not assist patients in harming themselves: "I will neither give a deadly drug to anybody if asked for it, nor will I make suggestion to this effect." Many physicians interpret the oath as prohibiting assisted suicide. Other opponents fear that allowing physician-assisted suicide will result in an epidemic of suicides and in the deaths of many people who are not ill but are only depressed. In addition, it may pressure some dying people into committing suicide when they would prefer to live. Leon R. Kass, an outspoken critic, states that once assisted suicide is legalized, it "will not remain confined to those who freely and knowingly elect it." Kass argues that ultimately there would be no effective controls and that society would head down a slippery slope to indiscriminate killing.

Physicians supporting assisted suicide, however, believe it is one way for doctors to address the concerns of patients who are terminally ill and near death. Two physicians, Christine K. Cassel and Diane E. Meier, write in the *New England Journal of Medicine* that patients who seek assistance to die "should not be held hostage to our inability or unwillingness to be responsible for knowing right from wrong." These physicians argue that the medical profession has ignored requests for death because it is unable to accept death and effectively deal with the dying. Derek Humphrey, founder of the right-to-die organization The Hemlock Society, states in his book *Final Exit* that death is an individual right of "personal autonomy concerning one's bodily integrity." He argues that a sensitive, caring society should allow people the option of assisted suicide so they can die as they choose.

Clearly, physician-assisted suicide is an emotion-filled issue that forces Americans to evaluate the needs of the dying and the role of the physician. The following chapter confronts the ethical and legal issues presented by physician-assisted suicide.

"It is not immoral for a physician to assist in the rational suicide of a terminally ill person. "

Physicians Can Ethically Assist in Suicide

Sidney H. Wanzer et al.

Sidney H. Wanzer is on the board of directors for the Society for the Right to Die, and is an associate physician at Harvard Law School Health Services in Cambridge, Massachusetts. In the following viewpoint, Wanzer and a panel of physicians conclude that applying certain criteria can make it ethical for a doctor to assist a terminally ill patient in committing suicide. The authors believe that hopelessly ill patients have a right to be free of pain and to have control of their medical treatment, including the right to control when and how they will die. Wanzer and a panel of physicians formulated this conclusion at a symposium sponsored by the Society for the Right to Die.

As you read, consider the following questions:

1. According to the authors, what is the difference between physician-assisted suicide and euthanasia?
2. Why does the panel emphasize the need for establishing doctor-patient collaboration?
3. What conditions does the panel say must exist for rational suicide to be acceptable?

Excerpted, with permission, from Sidney H. Wanzer et al., "The Physician's Responsibility Toward Hopelessly Ill Patients," *The New England Journal of Medicine* 320:13 (March 30, 1989), pp. 844-849.

Some of the practices that were controversial five years ago in the care of the dying patient have become accepted and routine. Do-not-resuscitate (DNR) orders, nonexistent only a few years ago, are now commonplace. Many physicians and ethicists now agree that there is little difference between nasogastric or intravenous hydration and other life-sustaining measures. They have concluded, therefore, that it is ethical to withdraw nutrition and hydration from certain dying, hopelessly ill, or permanently unconscious patients. The public and the courts have tended to accept this principle. Most important, there has been an increase in sensitivity to the desires of dying patients on the part of doctors, other health professionals, and the public. The entire subject is now discussed openly. Various studies and reports from governmental bodies, private foundations, the American Medical Association, and state medical societies reflect these advances in thinking. . . .

Legal, Medical, and Social Responses

The courts have continued to support patients' rights and have expanded the legal concept of the right to refuse medical treatment, upholding this right in more than 80 court decisions. As a general rule, the cases have involved terminally ill patients whose death was expected whether or not treatment was continued, and the treatment at issue . . . was often intrusive or burdensome. The courts recognized the patient's common-law right to autonomy (to be left alone to make one's own choices) as well as the constitutional right to privacy (to be protected from unwanted invasive medical treatment). . . .

Popular attitudes about the rights of dying patients have also changed, often in advance of the attitudes of health care providers, legislators, and the courts. The results of one public-opinion poll indicated that 68 percent of the respondents believed that "people dying of an incurable painful disease should be allowed to end their lives before the disease runs its course."

Health professionals have also become much more aware of patients' rights. In states with laws legitimizing living wills, hospitals have become responsive to patients' wishes as expressed in their advance directives, and hospital accreditation by the Joint Commission on Accreditation of Health Care Organizations now requires the establishment of formal DNR policies. The frequency with which DNR orders are used in nursing homes has also increased. In 1987 the California Department of Health Services became the first state agency to develop clear guidelines for the removal of life support, including tube feeding, in the state's 1500 nursing homes and convalescent hospitals. . . .

Physicians have a responsibility to consider timely discussions with patients about life-sustaining treatment and terminal care. Only a minority of physicians now do so consistently. The best time to begin such discussions is during the course of routine, nonemergency care, remembering that not all patients are emotionally prepared, by virtue of their stage in life, their psychological makeup, or the stage of their illness. Nevertheless, as a matter of routine, physicians should become acquainted with their patients' personal values and wishes and should document them just as they document information about medical history, family history, and sociocultural background. Such discussions and the resultant documentation should be considered a part of the minimal standard of acceptable care. The physician should take the initiative in obtaining the documentation and should enter it in the medical record. . . .

When Suicide Is Acceptable

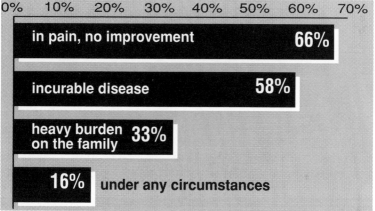

Response to the question: "In what circumstances does a person have a moral right to end his or her life?"

Source: 1990 Gallup Poll of 1,018 adults.

In general, health care institutions must recognize their obligation to inform patients of their right to participate in decisions about their medical care, including the right to refuse treatment, and should formulate institutional policies about the use of advance directives and the appointment of surrogate decision makers. Hospitals, health maintenance organizations, and nursing homes should ask patients on admission to indicate whether they have prepared a living will or designated a surrogate. It seems especially important that nursing homes require a regular review of patient preferences, with each patient's physician taking responsibility for ensuring that such information is obtained and documented. In the case of patients who lack decision-making capacity, surrogate decision makers should be identified and consulted appropriately. (We prefer the term "decision-making capacity" to "competency" because in the medical context, the patient either has or does not have the capacity to make decisions, whereas competency is a legal determination that can be made only by the courts.). . .

Pain and Suffering

The hopelessly ill patient must have whatever is necessary to control pain. One of the most pervasive causes of anxiety among patients, their families, and the public is the perception that physicians' efforts toward the relief of pain are sadly deficient. Because of this perceived professional deficiency, people fear that needless suffering will be allowed to occur as patients are dying. To a large extent, we believe such fears are justified.

A Right to Choose

I have been a longtime advocate of active, informed patient choice of treatment or nontreatment, and of a patient's right to die with as much control and dignity as possible. . . . Although I know we have measures to help control pain and lessen suffering, to think that people do not suffer in the process of dying is an illusion. Prolonged dying can occasionally be peaceful, but more often the role of the physician and family is limited to lessening but not eliminating severe suffering.

I wonder how many families and physicians secretly help patients over the edge into death in the face of such severe suffering. I wonder how many severely ill or dying patients secretly take their lives, dying alone in despair.

Timothy E. Quill, *The New England Journal of Medicine*, March 7, 1991.

In the patient whose dying process is irreversible, the balance between minimizing pain and suffering and potentially hastening death should be struck clearly in favor of pain relief. Narcotics or other pain medications should be given in whatever dose and by whatever route is necessary for relief. It is morally correct to increase the dose of narcotics to whatever dose is needed, even though the medication may contribute to the depression of respiration or blood pressure, the dulling of consciousness, or even death, provided the primary goal of the physician is to relieve suffering. The proper dose of pain medication is the dose that is sufficient to relieve pain and suffering, even to the point of unconsciousness. . . .

The principles of medical ethics are formulated independently of legal decisions, but physicians may fear that decisions about the care of the hopelessly ill will bring special risks of criminal charges and prosecution. Although no medical decision can be immune from legal scrutiny, courts in the United States have generally supported the approaches advocated here. The physician should follow these principles without exaggerated concern for legal consequences, doing whatever is necessary to relive pain and bring comfort, and adhering to the patient's wishes as much as possible. To withhold any necessary measure of pain relief in a hopelessly ill person out of fear of depressing respiration or of possible legal repercussions is unjustifiable. Good medical practice is the best protection against legal liability. . . .

If care is administered properly at the end of life, only the rare patient should be so distressed that he or she desires to commit suicide. Occasionally, however, all fails. The doctor, the nurse, the family, and the patient may have done everything possible to relieve the distress occasioned by a terminal illness, and yet the patient perceives his or her situation as intolerable and seeks assistance in bringing about death. Is it ever justifiable for the physician to assist suicide in such a case?

Some physicians, believing it to be the last act in a continuum of care provided for the hopelessly ill patient, to assist patients who request it, either by prescribing sleeping pills with knowledge of their intended use or by discussing the required doses and methods of administration with the patient. The frequency with which such actions are undertaken is unknown, but they are certainly not rare. Suicide differs from euthanasia in that the act of bringing on death is performed by the patient, not the physician.

Conditions Allowing Rational Suicides

The physician who considers helping a patient who requests assistance with suicide must determine first that the patient is indeed beyond all help and not merely suffering from a treatable depression of the sort common in people with terminal illnesses. Such a depression requires therapeutic intervention. If there is no treatable component to the depression and the patient's pain or suffering is refractory to treatment, then the wish for suicide may be rational. If such a patient acts on the wish for death and actually commits suicide, it is ethical for a physician who knows the patient well to refrain from an attempt at resuscitation.

Even though suicide itself is not illegal, helping a person commit suicide is a crime in many states, either by statute or under common law. Even so, we know of no physician who has ever been prosecuted in the United States for prescribing pills in order to help a patient commit suicide. However, the potential illegality of this act is a deterrent, and apart from that, some physicians simply cannot bring themselves to assist in suicide or to condone such action.

Complex Issues

Whether it is bad medical practice or immoral to help a hopelessly ill patient commit a rational suicide is a complex issue, provoking a number of considerations. First, as their disease advances, patients may lose their decision-making capacity because of the effects of the disease or the drug treatment. Assisting such patients with suicide comes close to performing an act of euthanasia. Second, patients who want a doctor's assistance with suicide may be unwilling to endure their terminal illness because they lack information about what is ahead. Even when the physician explains in careful detail the availability of flexible, continually adjusted care, the patient may still opt out of that treatment plan and reject the physician's efforts to ease the dying process. Also, what are the physician's obligations if a patient who retains decision-making capacity insists that family members not be told of a suicide plan? Should the physician insist on obtaining the family's consent? Finally, should physicians acknowledge their role in a suicide in some way—by obtaining consultation, or in writing? Physicians who act in secret become isolated and cannot consult colleagues or ethics committees for confirmation that the patient has made a rational decision. If contacted, such colleagues may well object and even consider themselves obligated to report the physician to the Board of Medical Licensure or to the prosecutor. The impulse to maintain secrecy gives the lie to the moral intuition that assistance with suicide is ethical.

It is difficult to answer such questions, but all but two of us (Jan van Eys and Edwin H. Cassem) believe that it is not immoral for a physician to assist in the rational suicide of a terminally ill person. However, we recognize that such an act represents a departure from the principle of continually adjusted care. . . . As such, it should be considered a separate alternative and not an extension of a flexible approach to care. . . . Clearly, the subject of assisted suicide deserves wide and open discussion.

"From the time of Hippocrates, the principles of medical ethics have instructed physicians to refuse their patients' requests for death-causing treatments."

Physicians Cannot Ethically Assist in Suicide

David Orentlicher

In the following viewpoint, David Orentlicher contends that assisting in the suicide of a patient contradicts the principles of medical ethics physicians have followed since the time of Hippocrates. Orentlicher believes that assisted suicide would create many ethical dilemmas and would eventually undermine the physician-patient relationship. While he supports a patient's right to voluntarily refuse treatment, he maintains that a doctor should not assist in the decision or the process. Orentlicher, an ethics and health policy attorney, develops legal and ethical policies for the American Medical Association.

As you read, consider the following questions:

1. What does Orentlicher state is the primary purpose of assisted suicide?
2. What concerns does the author have if physicians are allowed to assist in suicide?
3. How does the author distinguish assisted suicide from the voluntary withdrawal of life support?

David Orentlicher, "Physician Participation in Assisted Suicide," *Journal of the American Medical Association* 262:13 (October 6, 1991), pp. 1844-1845. © 1989, American Medical Association. Reprinted with permission.

Should a physician be able to assist the suicide of a hopelessly ill patient? A panel of distinguished physicians, brought together by the Society for the Right to Die and writing in the *New England Journal of Medicine*, says yes. Deeply rooted medical traditions and the guiding principles of medical practice, however, say no.

According to 10 of the panel's 12 members, if a hopelessly ill patient believes his or her condition is intolerable, then it should be permissible for a physician to provide the patient with the medical means and the medical knowledge to commit suicide. For example, the physician could prescribe sleeping pills for the patient and indicate how many pills there are in a lethal dose.

Society's Tolerance

Assisted suicide, then, differs from euthanasia in the extent to which the physician participates in the process. In assisted suicide, the patient performs the life-ending act under the physician's guidance, while in euthanasia, the physician administers the death-causing drug or other agent.

The panel's endorsement of assisted suicide appears to reflect an increasing willingness by society to condone assisted suicide or even euthanasia. In the Netherlands, for example, euthanasia under limited circumstances is practiced openly and commonly, with the support of the Dutch Medical Association, a government commission, and court decisions. Euthanasia is permitted in the Netherlands when four conditions are satisfied: there is intolerable suffering with no prospect of improvement; the patient is mentally competent to choose euthanasia; the patient requests euthanasia voluntarily, repeatedly, and consistently over a reasonable period of time; and two physicians, one of whom has not participated in the patient's care, agree that euthanasia is appropriate. According to estimates, 5000 to 10 000 of the Dutch die by euthanasia each year.

In the United States, anecdotal evidence suggests that assisted suicide is infrequently but increasingly being performed, particularly by patients with acquired immunodeficiency syndrome. In addition, public opinion polls indicate that the majority of Americans believe that assisted suicide should be permitted.

Society's increasing support for assisted suicide is demonstrated by trends in law enforcement. Even though assisted suicide is prohibited by law, there apparently have been no cases in which a physician was prosecuted for providing a patient with the medical means to take his or her own life.

Advocates of assisted suicide suggest that it is a natural extension of the principle that hopelessly ill patients may refuse life-prolonging medical care. However, assisted suicide is not easily justified by the concerns underlying that principle.

Society has increasingly recognized the right of hopelessly ill patients to decline life-sustaining treatments because these treatments often serve only to prolong suffering and because the right of personal autonomy entitles each person to decide for him or herself whether to accept medical care. Theoretically, these justifications could also support a hopelessly ill patient's right to commit suicide. Suicide would put an end to suffering that could be considered needless, and it would be a fulfillment of the patient's desires. However, it is quite another question whether the physician should provide the medical means to carry out the suicide.

Ordinarily, a physician provides medical care for two reasons: to sustain life and to relieve suffering. Occasionally, in the process of trying to sustain life or relieve suffering, a treatment may cause the patient to die. For example, a small percentage of patients will not survive coronary bypass surgery. Or, the dose of morphine necessary to ease pain in a terminally ill patient may impair the patient's ability to breathe. Performance of the surgery or administration of the morphine is nevertheless permissible because the primary purpose of the treatment is a valid one. In assisted suicide, on the other hand, the primary purpose of the treatment is to cause death. And, as recognized by the American Medical Association's Council on Ethical and Judicial Affairs, in its opinion on euthanasia, that purpose has no role in the professional responsibilities of the physicians. Indeed, from the time of Hippocrates, the principles of medical ethics have instructed physicians to refuse their patients' requests for death-causing treatments.

Number of Concerns

This long-standing rejection of assisted suicide reflects a number of concerns with assisted suicide. A patient contemplating assisted suicide will naturally want to discuss that possibility with his or her physician. If the physician appears sympathetic to the patient's interest in suicide, it may convey the impression that the physician feels assisted suicide is a desirable alternative. Such an impression may not be very comforting to the patient. Moreover, if the patient decides to reject suicide, will the patient have the same degree of confidence in the physician's commitment to his or her care as previously? In short, assisted suicide might seriously undermine an essential element of the patient-physician relationship, the patient's trust that the physician is wholeheartedly devoted to caring for the patient's health.

More troubling, as Prof Yale Kamisar has observed, is the possibility that the hopelessly ill patient will not feel entirely free to resist a suggestion from the physician that suicide would be appropriate, particularly since it comes from the person whose medical judgment the patient relies on. Patients who are enfeebled by disease and devoid of hope may choose assisted suicide not because they are really tired of life but because they think others are tired of them. Some patients, moreover, may feel an obligation to choose death to spare their families the emotional and financial burden of their care. Other patients may succumb to the repeated signals from society that it would prefer to spend its limited resources on other compelling needs.

Chuck Asay by permission of the *Colorado Springs Gazette Telegraph*.

Finally, assisted suicide is problematic in terms of its implementation. For many patients, the progression of disease will result in the impairment of decision-making capacity, either from the effects of the disease itself or those of drug treatment. Consequently, it may be difficult to ensure that a competent decision is being made. Even with competent patients, physicians may have trouble deciding whether a reliable decision has been made. At what point in the contemplation of suicide by the patient, for example, can the physician be confident that the patient has made a firm decision to end his or her life? What if the patient has changed his or her mind previously? Finally, the patient's apparently rational decision to commit suicide may reflect a mental depression that should be treated.

Not surprisingly, many of the arguments against assisted suicide could also be used to oppose the withdrawal of artificial life supports; the two have much in common. Nevertheless, for most people there is a clearly and viscerally felt distinction between acting to hasten death and refraining from delaying death.

An important explanation for the distinction lies in the fact that withdrawal of treatment permits death to take its natural course while assisted suicide short-circuits the dying process.

The distinction may also be articulated in terms of the relationship between the sick and those who try to help them. As Dr Leon Kass has written, physicians serve the needs of patients not because patients exercise self-determination but because patients are sick. Thus, for example, a patient may not insist on a treatment that the physician feels is inconsistent with sound medical practices. What the sick need and are entitled to seek from the efforts of physicians is health. Accordingly, physicians provide medical treatments to the sick to make them well, or as well as they can become. Treatment designed to bring on death, by definition, does not heal and is therefore fundamentally inconsistent with the physician's role in the patient-physician relationship.

The withdrawal of life support, on the other hand, does not violate the nature of the patient-physician relationship. While the physician has a duty to care for those who want to be healed, there should not be an obligation, or even an option, to impose treatment on those for whom it is unwelcome.

Practical Decisions

The distinction between acting to hasten death and refraining from delaying death also reflects an element of pragmatism. If patients were not entitled to refuse life-prolonging treatment, it would be difficult to define their corollary obligation to obtain medical care. Would a patient dying of cancer have to accept a regimen of chemotherapy that might prolong life for several months but would be painful, nauseating, and debilitating? Would patients have to remain hospitalized during the final stages of their illnesses if to return home to die would shorten their lives by days or weeks? If these obligations would not be appropriate, then there must be a right to decline at least some life-sustaining treatments. And, if that right exists, who, other than the patient, is in a position to assess whether the ability of a particular treatment to prolong life is outweighed by the burdens of the treatment?

Suicide by the hopelessly ill may someday be sanctioned. However, much more thought needs to be given before involving physicians in the process and compromising their essential role as healers.

"[The] medical profession has . . . been responsible for much unnecessary suffering and personal degradation by refusing to hasten a merciful death for pleading patients. "

Physician-Assisted Suicide Should Be Legal

Jack Kevorkian

Jack Kevorkian is a Michigan physician whose medical license was suspended after he assisted three women in committing suicide. In his book *Prescription: Medicide: The Goodness of Planned Death*, he argues that suicide should be a legally sanctioned option for terminally ill patients who rationally choose it. In this viewpoint, he proposes that physician-assisted suicide be legalized, and that "suicide centers" or "obitoriums" be established to give patients a place for a "serene, dignified death."

As you read, consider the following questions:

1. Why does the author say that doctors do not understand the Hippocratic oath?
2. What does Kevorkian believe physician-assisted suicide will prevent if it is legalized?
3. What name does Kevorkian give to the act of assisting in suicide when done by professional medical personnel?

Reprinted from Jack Kevorkian's *Prescription: Medicide* with permission of Prometheus Books, Buffalo, New York.

It seems almost self-evident today that death is the arch enemy of medicine, to be resisted incessantly with every weapon in its arsenal. Doctors justify this implacable enmity on the basis of the Hippocratic Oath, specifically on its stipulation that they keep their patients from harm and injustice. But that is an erroneous basis.

The real source of their misconstrued primary obligation lies not in the oath but in Section II of the Second Constitution of Hippocrates' treatise on epidemics. Physicians are exhorted by the father of their calling "to do good *or* to do no harm." A doctor's art entails the constellation of the disease, the patient, and himself; the doctor and his patient are to work together *to combat the disease.* Nowhere is it stated that the doctor must heroically lead his patient off to do battle with death.

Misguided Commitment

It is clear that as far as Hippocrates was concerned the main, indeed the *only*, enemy is disease—that is, the disturber of a person's "ease." And the means to fight that enemy is the art of medicine, the *servant* of which is the doctor (who today has instead made himself its lord). In having taken the tack of combating death, in thus having usurped a prerogative never advanced by its revered progenitor, the medical profession wantonly infringes both aspects of its special and genuinely Hippocratic obligation: In quixotically trying to conquer death, doctors all too frequently do no good for their patients' "ease"; but, at the same time, they do harm instead by prolonging and even magnifying patients' dis-ease.

This monomaniacal and ultimately foolish obsession with subduing death is one side of the same coin. The other side is medicine's equally misguided commitment to maintaining life at all costs (which comprises a fairly large chunk of our gross national product). This contrived obligation serves as the basis of an implied commandment for doctors not to purposely kill any human being, and therefore to reject euthanasia or mercy killing.

As another "official and incontrovertible" justification for that commandment, doctors point to this short sentence in the oath: "I will neither give a deadly drug to anybody if asked for it, nor will I make a suggestion to this effect." Therefore, for them euthanasia is absolutely unethical. This may be true for a good number of today's doctors, but it wasn't always so, not even in Hippocrates' day. . . .

Hopelessly tied to a misinterpretation of the oath, a misguided medical profession has for centuries been responsible for much unnecessary suffering and personal degradation by refusing to hasten a merciful death for pleading patients. To me it is incredible that a doctor could abide the agony of a doomed human simply because of a personal commitment to an invented abstraction, be it mere opinion or some exalted principle born of cogitation. As philosopher Samuel Gorowitz states, the price of a doctor steadfastly adhering to his own personal convictions in refusing to aid or perform euthanasia is not extracted from his or her own life, but is thereby imposed on the suffering patient who professes a different set of values. "Thus," chides Gorowitz, "(the doctor) becomes one whose values demand behavior that results in the impoverishment in the lives of others, and which therefore will be seen by many to be parochial, inhumane, and unjustified.". . .

Joel Pett/*Lexington Herald-Leader*. Reprinted with permission.

Euthanasia wasn't of much interest to me until my internship year, when I saw first-hand how cancer can ravage the human body. The patient was a helplessly immobile woman of middle age, her entire body jaundiced to an intense yellow-brown, skin stretched paper-thin over a fluid-filled abdomen swollen to four or five times normal size. The rest of her was an emaciated skeleton: sagging, discolored skin covered her bones like a cheap, wrinkled frock.

The poor wretch stared up at me with yellow eyeballs sunken in their atrophic (withering) sockets. Her yellow teeth were ringed by chapping and parched lips to form an involuntary, almost sardonic "smile" of death. It seemed as though she was pleading for help and death at the same time. Out of sheer empathy alone I could have helped her die with satisfaction. From that moment on, I was sure that doctor-assisted euthanasia and suicide are and always were ethical, no matter what anyone says or thinks. . . .

Legal Consequences

Depending on the state or political entity and the law enforcement personalities involved, a doctor who performs euthanasia in the United States faces a spectrum of unpredictable penalties, ranging from none at all, through suspended sentence, probation, limited incarceration, life imprisonment, and—theoretically only—a death sentence. Of course, the charge of murder is absurd. . . . Under current state laws the only admissible charge for having committed active euthanasia would be voluntary manslaughter, meaning the actual performance of the willful and unlawful killing of a human being without malice, either express or implied (in contrast to the passive euthanasia of merely letting die). These crazy-quilt legal distinctions in America make it dangerous and even deadly for some doctors to do what they know is right.

The tragic case of Dr. John Kraai is a good example. In 1985 the seventy-six-year-old general practitioner in a town near Rochester, New York, was charged with second degree murder for having injected a lethal dose of insulin into his eighty-one-year-old nursing home patient suffering from Alzheimer's disease and gangrene of the feet. The old man had been Kraai's patient for over forty years. Many of the doctor's other patients rallied to his support. To their dismay he was found dead shortly afterwards, apparently due to a self-injected drug. The president of the local county medical society lamented the "sorry end to a long career of service for a man who spent his entire life taking care of people." But it should not be forgotten that Kraai's own profession was indirectly responsible for that sorry end. . . .

Taking a Risk

I decided to take the risky step of assisting terminal patients in committing suicide. I could not even consider performing active euthanasia and thereby being charged with murder in a very hostile milieu. Merely helping with self-killing would entail less risk. It would also help clarify the law.

The legal befuddlement is there for all to see. Fortunately, the old common law condemnation of suicide as a crime has been rescinded. Suicide, attempted or successful, is no longer a criminal act. How, then, can *assisting* someone to perform that legal act be called criminal and illegal? But that sort of blatant irrationality is incorporated into the laws of at least thirty of our states, and therefore makes assisted suicide a risky action, too. When word of my plans reached the county prosecutor's office, I was threatened with the possible charge of first degree murder (of all things!) if I helped patients die—despite my protest that aiding a suicide can never be murder. . . .

The prosecutor's empty threat could not deter me, because in the final analysis I would not be inciting suicide. In fact, like the Dutch euthanasists I would even try talking patients out of taking their own lives, and then assist them only as a last resort.

The first step was to decide on the method I was to use. Supplying drugs for the patient to swallow would be too much like active euthanasia. Then I recalled that in our medical school lectures on pathology the professor somewhat cynically remarked that carbon monoxide offers the best way to commit suicide. The pure gas has no color, taste, or smell; and it's toxic enough to cause rapid unconsciousness in relatively low concentration. . . .

Therefore, I intended to advise patients and their families on where to obtain the gas and how it was to be administered under my supervision. A thin plastic tube would connect a small gas canister or tank to a routine plastic mask over the patient's nose and mouth, as routinely done in hospitals for oxygen therapy. I would attach ECG [electrocardiogram] electrodes to the patient to monitor heart action. The gas would be turned on by the patient at a time of his or her choosing, with the rate of flow previously adjusted to cause death in about five minutes—to be verified by the ECG tracing. . . .

Changing Public Perceptions

I am convinced that the mere availability of euthanasia and physician-assisted suicide will avert the panic known to motivate many apparently senseless suicides. Furthermore, it is conceivable that in the future the accumulated experience of many years underlying a well-established, tightly controlled, and finely honed program of euthanasia will afford a reliable and objective gauge for distinguishing potentially irrational suicide. After all, would anyone in his or her right mind prefer to contemplate self-destruction with other conventional and certainly less pleasant means, and under less than optimal circumstances? . . .

Euthanasia is and always has been a purely negative concept, no matter how it's done or what qualifying label is put on it. I am trying to persuade society to turn it around into something positive. I believe that death . . . can be merciful and at the same time yield something of real value to the suffering humanity left behind.

The medical profession's single-minded obsession with the longevity of life has blinded it to other special needs of society and has spawned the inevitable ethical dilemmas now upon us. Rapidly changing socioeconomic and demographic conditions will soon force the intransigent medical profession to accept planned death by euthanasia, even if only of the negative kind. Then the profession would be doing the right thing, but for the wrong reason: it would have acted only because it was forced to do so.

Accepting Planned Death

The time has come to smash the last irrational and most fearsome taboo of planned death and thereby to open the floodgates of equally momentous benefit for humankind.

Jack Kevorkian, *Prescription: Medicide: The Goodness of Planned Death*, 1991.

The right thing and the right reason for doing it were advocated in France back in 1919, but fell on deaf ears throughout the world. Perhaps only because the need for it then wasn't plain for all to see, nobody took seriously Dr. Binet-Sangle's farsighted proposal for the establishment of professionally staffed and well-equipped "suicide centers" for the sole purpose of assuring a humane and painless death for all those who need and desire it. The time has come not only to consider his idea but to make the "quantum leap" of supplementing merciful killing with the enormously positive benefit of experimentation and organ donation. . . .

Legalized Suicide Centers

Research activity at the fringes of law and morality could be centralized, rationally organized, well controlled, and ethically validated in official "suicide centers" created specifically for the good of moribund subjects by affording them a serene, dignified death as well as a proper atmosphere for completely ethical manipulations. The latter objectives, such as getting their organs and doing experiments on them, would then be above reproach. They would be entirely ethical spinoffs of the main aim if pursued within well-reasoned and solidly inculcated guidelines and sensible legislation. This open and formal approach would also minimize the probability of abuse.

It should be obvious that the envisioned innovative by-products of mercy killing call for new terms to distinguish them from what is traditionally known as euthanasia, which now is not the simple concept it once was. Therefore, I propose that the term "euthanasia" be restricted to denote the termination of life performed by anybody. If performed only by professional medical personnel (such as a doctor, nurse, paramedic, physician's assistant, or medical technologist), then it becomes *medicide*.

Such a unique "suicide center" as described above obviously would offer society more than empty, negative death. Its much more important *positive* mission calls for a name worthy of that noble purpose. Because "suicide" and "euthanasia" have ineradicably negative connotations, I coined the word *obitorium* (from the Latin *obitus*, meaning "to go to meet death") for the center, and *obitiatry* (pronounced oh-bit-eye-a-tree, and using *iatros* meaning "doctor" in Greek) for the specialty. Logically its practitioner would then be an obitiatrist.

Therefore, obitiatry is the name of the medical specialty concerned with the treatment or doctoring of death to achieve some sort of beneficial result, in the same way that psychiatry is the name of the medical specialty concerned with the treatment or doctoring of the psyche for the beneficial result of mental health. In other words, medicide is euthanasia, but euthanasia may not be medicide. And obitiatry is medicide, but medicide may not be obitiatry.

The time has come to let medicide extend a comforting hand to those slipping into the valley of death, and to let obitiatry extract from their ebbing vitality the power to illuminate some of its darkest recesses for those who come after them.

"What begins as a right of doctors to kill under specified conditions will soon become a duty to kill."

Physician-Assisted Suicide Should Not Be Legal

Daniel Callahan

Daniel Callahan is the cofounder and director of the Hastings Center in Briarcliff Manor, New York, a research and educational organization that examines ethical issues in medicine. Callahan, a well-known and respected medical ethicist, opposes the legalization of physician-assisted suicide. In the following viewpoint, he states that making physician-assisted suicide legal will have terrible consequences for doctors and their patients. Ill patients would feel pressured into committing suicide, and gradually even those who are suicidal but not ill would expect assistance from physicians. These consequences, Callahan concludes, would harm the physician-patient relationship.

As you read, consider the following questions:

1. What does the author mean when he says physician-assisted suicide is not a personal act between a doctor and a patient?
2. Why does Callahan maintain that the argument of those in favor of physician-assisted suicide is fatally flawed?
3. What are the negative social consequences of legalized physician-assisted suicide, according to the author?

Adapted, with permission, from Daniel Callahan's "'Aid-in-Dying': The Social Dimensions," *Commonweal*, August 9, 1991, © 1991 Commonweal Foundation.

The fear of dying is powerful. Even more powerful sometimes is the fear of not dying, of being forced to endure destructive pain, or to live out a life of unrelieved, pointless suffering. The movement to legalize euthanasia and assisted suicide is a strong and, seemingly, historically inevitable response to that fear. It draws part of its strength from the failure of modern medicine to reassure us that it can manage our dying with dignity and comfort. It draws another part from the desire to be masters of our fate. Why must we endure that which need not be endured? If medicine cannot always bring us the kind of death we might like through its technical skills, why can it not use them to give us a quick and merciful release? Why can we not have "aid-in-dying"? . . .

Individual Right

Exactly a century ago, in the 1891 *Union Pacific* v. *Bostford* case, the Supreme Court held that "No right is more sacred, or is more carefully guarded, by the common law, than the right of the individual to the possession and control of his own person." That right has been reaffirmed time and again, and especially underscored in those rulings that declare our right to terminate medical treatment and thus to die.

But if it should happen to be impossible for us to so easily bring about our own death, would it not be reasonable to ask someone else, specifically a doctor, to help us to die? Would it not, moreover, be an act of mercy for a doctor to give us that kind of a release? Is not the relief of suffering a high moral good?

To say "no" in response to questions of that kind seems both repressive and cruel. They invoke our cherished political values of liberty and self-determination. They draw upon our deep and long-standing moral commitment to the relief of suffering. They bespeak our ancient efforts to triumph over death, to find a way to bring it to heel.

Nonetheless, we should as a society say no, and decisively so, to euthanasia and assisted suicide. . . . If a death marked by pain or suffering is a nasty death, a natural biological evil of a supreme kind, euthanasia and assisted suicide are wrong and harmful responses to that evil. To directly kill another person in the name of mercy (as I will define "euthanasia" here), or to assist another to commit suicide (which seems to me logically little different from euthanasia) would add to a society already burdened with man-made evils still another. . . .

Dire Social Consequences

Legalization would also provide an important social sanction for euthanasia, affecting many aspects of our society beyond the immediate relief of suffering individuals. The implications of that sanction are profound. It would change the traditional role of the physician. It would require the regulation and oversight of government. It would add to the acceptable range of permissible killing in our society still another occasion for one person to take the life of another.

No Right to Suicide

If suicide is a right, then it is one that has remained undiscovered throughout the ages by the great thinkers in law, ethics, philosophy and theology. It appears nowhere in the Bible or the Koran or the Talmud. Committing suicide wasn't a "right" a 1,000 years ago, and it isn't one now. That's why most societies—including our own—have passed laws against it. The two women who went to Dr. Kevorkian and took a strong dose of his hemlock were fully aware of the consequences of their actions. Now Dr. Kevorkian must take the legal consequences of his.

The Washington Times, October 30, 1991.

We might decide that we are as a people prepared to live with those implications. But we should not deceive ourselves into thinking of euthanasia or assisted suicide as merely personal acts, just a slight extension of the already-established right to control our bodies and to have medical treatment terminated. It is a radical move into an entirely different realm of morality: that of the killing of one person by another. . . .

Historical Perspectives

Traditionally, only three circumstances have been acceptable for the taking of life: killing in self-defense or to protect another life, killing in the course of a just war, and, in the case of capital punishment, killing by agents of the state. Killing in both war and capital punishment has been opposed by some, and most successfully in the case of capital punishment, now banned in many countries, particularly those of Western Europe.

Apart from those long-standing debates, what is most notable about the historically licit conditions of killing is (1) the requirement that killing is permissible only when relatively objective standards have been met (in war or self-defense, a genuine threat to life or vital goods, and the absence of an alternative means of meeting those threats); and (2) when the public good is thereby served. (Even in self-defense, the permission to kill has some element of fostering a sense of public security in the face of personal threats.). . .

The law does not now allow, in the United States or elsewhere, the right of one person to kill another even if the latter requests, or consents, that it be done. All civilized societies have also outlawed private killings, either in the name of honor (dueling, for instance), or to right private wrongs (to revenge adulterous relationships, for instance).

Yet if we generally accept in our society a right to control our own life and body, why has the extension of that right to private killing been denied? The most obvious reason is a reluctance to give one person absolute and irrevocable power over the life of another, whether there is consent or not. That prohibition is a way of saying that the social stakes in the legitimization of killing are extraordinarily high. It is to recognize that a society should—for the mutual protection of all—be exceedingly parsimonious about conferring a right to kill on anyone, for whatever reason. . . .

Fatally Flawed

We come here to a striking pitfall of the common argument for euthanasia and assisted suicide. Once the key premises of that argument are accepted, there will remain no logical way in the future to: (1) deny euthanasia to anyone who requests it for whatever reason, terminal illness or not; or to (2) deny it to the suffering incompetent, even if they do not request it. We can erect legal safeguards and specify required procedures to keep that from happening. But over time they will provide poor protection if the logic of the moral premises upon which they are based are fatally flawed.

Where are the flaws here? Recall that there are two classical arguments in favor of euthanasia and assisted suicide: our right of self-determination, and our claim upon the mercy of others, especially doctors, to relieve our suffering if they can do so. These two arguments are typically spliced together and presented as a single contention. Yet if they are considered independently—and there is no inherent reason why they must be linked—they display serious problems. Consider, first, the argument for our right of self-determination. It is said that a competent, adult person should have a right to euthanasia for the relief of suffering. But why must the person be suffering? Does not that stipulation already compromise the right of self-determination? How can self-determination have any limits? Why are not the person's desires or motives, whatever they may be, sufficient? How can we justify this arbitrary limitation of self-determination? The standard arguments for euthanasia offer no answers to those questions.

Consider next the person who is suffering but not competent, who is perhaps demented or mentally retarded. The standard argument . . . would deny euthanasia to that person. But why? If a person is suffering but not competent, then it would seem grossly unfair to deny relief simply because that person lacks competence. Are the incompetent less entitled to relief from suffering than the competent? Will it only be affluent middle-class people, mentally fit and able, who can qualify? Will those who are incompetent but suffering be denied that which those who are intellectually and emotionally better off can have? Would that be fair? Do they suffer less for being incompetent? The standard argument about our duty to relieve suffering offers no response to those questions either.

Jerry-Rigged Combination

Is it, however, fair to euthanasia advocates to do what I have done, to separate, and treat individually, the two customary arguments in favor of a legal right to euthanasia? The implicit reason for so joining them is no doubt the desire to avoid abuse. By requiring a showing of suffering and terminal illness, the aim is to exclude perfectly healthy people from demanding that, in the name of self-determination and for their own private reasons, another person can be called upon to kill them. By requiring a show of mental competence to effect self-determination, the aim is to exclude the nonvoluntary killing of the depressed, the retarded, and the demented.

My contention is that the joining of those two requirements is perfectly arbitrary, a jerry-rigged combination if ever there was one. Each has its own logic, and each could be used to justify euthanasia. But in the nature of the case that logic, it seems evident, offers little resistance to denying any competent person the right to be killed, sick or not; and little resistance to killing the incompetent, so long as there is good reason to believe they are suffering. There is no principled reason to reject that logic, and no reason to think it could long remain suppressed by the expedient of arbitrary legal stipulations. . . .

Justifying Moral Grounds

The doctor will not be able to use a medical standard. He or she will only be able to use a moral standard. Faced with a patient reporting great suffering, a doctor cannot, therefore, justify euthanasia on purely medical grounds (because suffering is unmeasurable and scientifically undiagnosable). To maintain professional and personal integrity, the doctor will have to justify it on his or her own moral grounds. The doctor must believe that a life of subjectively experienced intense suffering is not worth living. He must believe that himself if he is to be justified in taking the decisive and ultimate step of killing the patient: it must be his moral reason to act, not the patient's reason (even though they may coincide). But if he believes that a life of some forms of suffering is not worth living, then how can he deny the same relief to a person who cannot request it, or who requests it but whose competence is in doubt? This is simply a different way of making the point that there is no self-evident reason why the supposed duty to relieve suffering must be limited to competent patients claiming self-determination. Or why patients who claim death as their right under self-determination must be either suffering or dying.

A Right to Choose

I have been a longtime advocate of active, informed patient choice of treatment or nontreatment, and of a patient's right to die with as much control and dignity as possible. . . .

Although I know we have measures to help control pain and lessen suffering, to think that people do not suffer in the process of dying is an illusion. Prolonged dying can occasionally be peaceful, but more often the role of the physician and family is limited to lessening but not eliminating severe suffering.

I wonder how many families and physicians secretly help patients over the edge into death in the face of such severe suffering. I wonder how many severely ill or dying patients secretly take their lives, dying alone in despair.

Timothy E. Quill, *The New England Journal of Medicine*, March 7, 1991.

There is, moreover, the possibility that what begins as a right of doctors to kill under specified conditions will soon become a duty to kill. On what grounds could a doctor deny a request by a competent person for euthanasia? It will not do, I think, just to specify that no doctor should be required to do that which violates her conscience. As commonly articulated, the argument about why a doctor has a right to perform euthanasia—the dual duty to respect patient self-determination and to relieve suffering—is said to be central to the vocation of being a doctor. Why should duties as weighty as those be set aside on the grounds of "conscience" or "personal values"?

These puzzles make clear that the moral situation is radically changed once our self-determination requires the participation and assistance of a doctor. It is then that doctor's moral life, that doctor's integrity, that is also and no less encompassed in the act of euthanasia. What, we might then ask, should be the appropriate moral standards for a person asked to kill another? What are the appropriate virtues and sensitivities of such a person? How should that person think of his or her own life and find, within that life, a place for the killing of another person? The language of a presumed right of someone to kill another to relieve suffering obscures questions of that kind. . . .

Our duty to relieve suffering cannot justify the introduction of new evils into society. The risk of doing just that in the legalization of "aid-in-dying" is too great, particularly since the number of people whose pain and suffering could not be relieved would never be a large one (so even most euthanasia advocates recognize). It is too great because it would take a disproportionate social change to bring it about, one whose implications extend far beyond the sick and dying. It is too great because, as the history of the twentieth century should demonstrate, killing is a contagious disease, not easy to stop once unleashed in society. It is too great a risk because it would offer medicine too convenient a way out of its hardest cases, those where there is ample room for further, more benign reforms. We are far from exhausting the known remedies for the relief of pain (frequently, even routinely, underused), and a long way from providing decent psychological support for those who suffer from despair and a sense of futility in continuing life.

Pain and suffering in the critically ill and dying are great evils. The attempt to relieve them by the introduction of euthanasia and assisted suicide is even greater. Those practices threaten the future security of the living. They no less threaten the dying themselves. Once a society allows one person to take the life of another based on their mutual private standards of a life worth living, there can be no safe or sure way to contain the deadly virus thus introduced. It will go where it will thereafter.

Understanding Words in Context

Readers occasionally come across words they do not recognize. And frequently, because they do not know a word or words, they will not fully understand the passage being read. Obviously, the reader can look up an unfamiliar word in a dictionary. By carefully examining the word in the context in which it is used, however, the word's meaning can often be determined. A careful reader may find clues to the meaning of the word in surrounding words, ideas, and attitudes.

Below are excerpts from the viewpoints in this chapter. In each excerpt, one of the words is printed in italics. Try to determine the meaning of each word by reading the excerpt. Under each excerpt you will find four definitions for the italicized word. Choose the one that is closest to your understanding of the word.

Finally, use a dictionary to see how well you have understood the words in context. It will be helpful to discuss with others the clues that helped you decide on each word's meaning.

1. Some people have appointed a person to express their wishes about medical treatment in case they are too ill to speak for themselves. That is why many hospitals now ask patients on admission to indicate if they have designated a *SURROGATE*.

   SURROGATE means:

   a) lawyer   c) doctor
   b) substitute   d) driver

2. Physicians realize that they have a responsibility for all of the care their terminally ill patients receive. Some believe that assisted suicide is the last act in a *CONTINUUM* of care provided for such patients.

   CONTINUUM means:

   a) range   c) analysis
   b) agreement   d) breakdown

3. Medication does not always ease the torment of terminally ill patients. In such cases, when the patient's pain and suffering is *REFRACTORY* to treatment, the wish for suicide may be rational.

REFRACTORY means:

a) manageable
b) responsive
c) resistant
d) agreeable

4. There are numerous personal tales of events where caretakers and doctors have assisted patients to commit suicide. These *ANECDOTES* suggest that assisted suicide is infrequently but increasingly being performed.

ANECDOTES means:

a) lists of facts
b) brief stories
c) home movies
d) theories of death

5. Patients who are slowed down by disease sometimes feel they are a burden to those taking care of them. Such patients, who are *ENFEEBLED* by disease, may choose assisted suicide not because they are really tired of life but because they think others are tired of them.

ENFEEBLED means:

a) transported
b) enthused
c) strengthened
d) weakened

6. Supporters of assisted suicide believe it is simply *PRAGMATIC* for a doctor to disconnect the life-support system of a patient who is clearly going to die anyway.

PRAGMATIC means:

a) practical
b) wrong
c) believeable
d) illegal

7. Humans are constantly trying to use medical technology to keep themselves and others alive. These attempts *BESPEAK* our ancient efforts to triumph over death.

BESPEAK means:

a) endanger
b) indicate
c) criticize
d) magnify

8. There are a few instances when the law allows one person to kill another. These *LICIT* conditions of killing have usually been limited to war and self-defense.

LICIT means:

a) legal
b) distasteful
c) understood
d) moral

Periodical Bibliography

The following articles have been selected to supplement the diverse views presented in this chapter.

George J. Annas — "Killing Machines: Doctors and Suicide," *Hastings Center Report*, March/April 1991.

Christine K. Cassel and Diane E. Meier — "Morals and Moralism in the Debate over Euthanasia and Assisted Suicide," *The New England Journal of Medicine*, September 13, 1990. Available from PO Box 803, Waltham, MA 02254-0803.

Richard Doerflinger — "Assisted Suicide: Pro-Choice or Anti-Life?" *Hastings Center Report*, January 2, 1989.

Gavin Fairbairn — "Enforced Death: Enforced Life," *Journal of Medical Ethics*, September 1991.

Daniel Goleman — "Depression's Grip on Terminal Cases," *The New York Times*, December 4, 1991.

Daniel Gross — "Don't Block the Exit," *Reason*, April 1990.

Issues — "Assisted Suicide: The Moving Case of Diane Raises Serious Questions," March/April 1991. Available from managing editor, 477 N. Lindbergh Blvd., St. Louis, MO 63141.

Issues — "Patient Self-Determination Act: How Will It Affect Informed Consent?" September/October 1991.

Leon R. Kass — "Why Doctors Must Not Kill," *Commonweal*, August 9, 1991.

Jon G. Murray — "Body and Soul: The Euthanasia Question," *American Atheist*, vol. 33, no. 4, April 1991.

Timothy Quill — "A Case of Individualized Decision Making," *The New England Journal of Medicine*, March 7, 1991.

Ramsey Colloquium — "Always to Care, Never to Kill: A Declaration on Euthanasia," *First Things*, February 1992. Available from PO Box 3000, Dept. FT, Denville, NJ 07834.

Benson B. Roe — "Physician Attitudes About Death," *Pharos*, Winter 1991. Available from Carolyn L. Kuckein, 525 Middlefield Rd., Suite 130, Menlo Park, CA 94025.

Cheryl K. Smith — "Legal Review: Informed Consent—A Shift from Paternalism to Self-Determination," *Topics in Health Record Management*, September 1990. Available from Aspen Publishers, Inc., 1600 Research Blvd., Rockville, MD 20850.

What Are the Causes of Teen Suicide?

Chapter Preface

In the book *The Enigma of Suicide*, George Howe Colt narrates the stories of two teenage boys. Justin Spoonhour, physically unkempt, quiet, and an outcast, did not participate in many social or sports activities. Brian Hart, handsome, athletic, and outgoing, involved himself with people and activities. Yet the boys had one thing in common—they both committed suicide. Why?

Friends and relatives speculate as to what might have driven these two boys to kill themselves. Justin made attempts to be accepted socially but was considered a misfit by his peers. He never told anyone that he was unhappy about being an outsider. He was never involved with drugs or alcohol and had no history of psychiatric problems. Yet on Valentine's Day 1984, when students exchanged flowers, Justin did not receive a flower. Those who knew him speculate that this rejection led him to kill himself that day.

Brian experienced two traumas as a child: He witnessed a friend's eye shot out with a BB rifle, and he saw his dog hit by a train. Brian did become involved with drugs and alcohol and had psychiatric problems. His parents speculate that his manic depression drove him to suicide and that the childhood traumas had exacerbated his depression. Even with these speculations, however, no one really knows what led Justin or Brian to choose to commit suicide.

In the quest to answer the question of why teenagers choose to kill themselves and perhaps to prevent other teens from committing suicide, psychologists, doctors, sociologists, ethicists, and writers have proposed a variety of explanations. They often blame the stress of living in today's society, drugs and alcohol, or the lack of family and religious support. While most experts focus on specific biological, sociological, or psychological causes, others argue that the reasons for suicide are as individual as teenagers themselves.

Understanding the motivation behind teen suicide may help society identify teens who are at risk and stop them from killing themselves. The following chapter discusses possible causes for teen suicide.

"Stress resulting from . . . major life changes undoubtedly taxes the adolescent's coping skills and contributes to the rates of suicide."

Stress Causes Teen Suicide

Judith M. Stillion, Eugene E. McDowell, and Jacque H. May

In the following viewpoint, Judith M. Stillion, Eugene E. McDowell, and Jacque H. May contend that many adolescents face mental, physical, and social challenges that may overwhelm them and lead to suicide. The authors believe that some teenagers fail to develop the proper skills to cope with the anxieties of growing up. Stillion, a professor at Western Carolina University in Cullowhee, North Carolina, has written extensively about suicide. McDowell, director of the Asheville Graduate Center of the University of North Carolina, has written books and given presentations on youth suicide. May has a master's degree in clinical psychology.

As you read, consider the following questions:

1. What do the authors characterize as the "common adolescent complaint"?
2. What are Erik Erikson's two stages of personality development for adolescents, according to the authors?
3. What are the stresses that adolescents face, according to the authors?

Excerpted from *Suicide Across the Life Span: Premature Exits* by Judith M. Stillion, Eugene E. McDowell, and Jacque H. May. Philadelphia: Hemisphere Books, 1989. Reprinted with permission from Hemisphere Books, a member of the Taylor & Francis Group.

So much of adolescence is an ill-defined dying,
An intolerable waiting,
A longing for another place and time,
Another condition.

Theodore Roethke, *I'm Here*

The phenomenon of suicide in adolescence and young adulthood has received much attention in recent years. Newspaper
articles, books, and research reports have attempted to explain
the rapid increase in suicidal behavior among people in these
age groups. However, as A. Berman and T. Carroll have pointed
out, the literature on youth suicide has many weaknesses. Most
of these weaknesses are inherent in the subject itself and apply
to all age groups. For example, it is impossible to study suicide
from the point of view of those who commit it, since they are
dead. This means that most of our knowledge about completed
suicide is gathered retrospectively and from secondary sources.
Even with improved methods for carrying out psychological au-
topsies (post-suicide studies), results of such research must be
interpreted cautiously. In addition to the problems of carrying
out research on completed suicides, there is growing evidence
that the acts of attempted and completed suicide may have different meanings. Suicidal acts vary in lethality from mere gestures to completed suicide, yet the research literature rarely
controls for the level of lethality among attempters.

Understanding Types of Behavior

Berman has suggested that there are several types of adolescents who are at high risk for engaging in suicidal behavior, including "the affectively disordered, the substance abusing, the
conduct disordered, the rigid perfectionist, and the socially
marginal." However, individual types of behavior among suicidal youth have rarely been studied in depth. Intentionality has
also rarely been studied. Attempters who never meant to die are
grouped with those whose only desire is to die. Researchers
tend to use different definitions of the term *suicidal* and frequently do not clearly operationalize them, making comparisons
between studies difficult. Much of the research on youth suicide
does not include comparison groups, making it difficult to know
if the findings of the study apply only to suicide attempters or if
they also apply to nonsuicidal youth. . . .

In order to understand suicidal individuals, it is necessary to
know about the normative events of the period of life in which
these individuals are attempting to function. . . .

The rapid, asynchronous (uneven) growth in adolescence, coupled with the effect of relatively high levels of hormones, causes

both boys and girls to become more self-conscious and intro-spective than they were in childhood. They focus on their changing body image and often develop negative feelings about themselves. This restricted focus can feed into a rise in adoles-cent egocentrism, which may result in adolescents' feeling unique, misunderstood, and lonely. The common adolescent complaint—"No one understands me"—is evidence of the kind of idiosyncratic emotions that may play a role in the rising sui-cide statistics among adolescents. . . .

Stress and Today's Teenagers

The increase in the teenage-suicide rate over the past quarter century may reflect the increase in stress contemporary young people experience. Today's teenagers face problems that are dif-ferent from those faced by teens of previous generations. They have more freedom—to engage in sexual activity and to abuse drugs. They experience more loss due to the soaring divorce rate. And on another level, young people today also have lost the sense of progress, that the world is getting better.

David Elkind, *Parents*, January 1990.

The period of adolescence is considered to be formally over when the individual has become an independent adult and be-gins to function on his or her own without the help of parents. The period of adolescence has lengthened in the United States during this century. Puberty now occurs 2 years earlier for both boys and girls than it did at the turn of the century. In addition, many young people remain in college for a longer period of time or return home after college, thus re-entering the semidepen-dent world of adolescence. (The fact that the period of depen-dency has lengthened at the upper end in recent years lends support to our decision to define adolescence as the period from 15 to 24 years of age.)

Sexual Awareness

In the area of psychological growth, according to psychoana-lytic theory, adolescents are in the final stage of personality de-velopment, the genital stage. Because Freud strongly believed that the early years are more important than later years in per-sonality development, less has been written about the genital stage than any other. During the genital stage, in response to in-creased hormones, the libidinal drives reappear after the hiber-nation of the latency period, and sexual motivation and activity take on more adult forms. The adolescent seeks more adult sex-ual experiences, in dramatic contrast to the preference for one's own sex which characterized the preceding stage.

The healthy adolescent enters the adult sexual world through a variety of group experiences involving both boys and girls. Then group experiences gradually give way to deeper and more exclusive relationships with a member of the opposite sex. According to psychoanalytic theory, the poorly adjusted adolescent brings many unresolved problems from earlier stages of development into the genital period. Early conflicts related to trust (from the oral stage), difficulty with authority (from the anal stage), or sexual identification problems (from the phallic stage) all have specific implications for adult personality. . . . When the adolescent must expend too much energy in repressing or otherwise defending against problems from earlier stages, the balance between eros and thanatos is disturbed; this creates the possibility for the strengthening of death wishes, which are sometimes manifested in suicidal behavior.

Identity Versus Role Diffusion

In contrast to Freud, who showed relatively little interest in this age group, Erik Erikson described personality development in adolescence in great detail. Erikson proposed two stages of personality development for this age group: (1) identity versus role diffusion, for young adolescents, and (2) intimacy versus isolation, for older adolescents and young adults.

Young adolescents in the stage of identity versus role diffusion struggle to determine who they are and who they want to become while at the same time experiencing major physical changes and the development of adultlike sexual interests. They must synthesize what they have learned about themselves during the preceding 12 to 14 years and incorporate the rapid physical and psychological changes of adolescence into an understanding of self (or self-concept) which will be an important part of their adult personality.

Adolescents typically cope with this struggle toward identity by turning to peers, popular heroes, and causes. They usually engage in a process of trying out various ways of being under the critical eyes of their peers. Successful adolescents gradually glean a growing sense of identity through this trial and error process. Unsuccessful ones become involved in the cliquish and critical world of adolescence without being able to discern what can and cannot be incorporated into their growing sense of self. As these individuals grow older they continue to show the clannishness and intolerance of adolescence. They remain confused concerning their identity and their role in life, and they are not prepared to meet the challenges of adulthood. They are likely to fail in the adult responsibilities of intimacy and generativity and to suffer low self-esteem and depression (which has repeatedly been associated with suicide).

Recognizing Suicidal Teenagers

Learn to recognize the signs of serious depression and suicide risk. Eight out of ten suicides give definite warnings, verbal or behavioral, of their intentions:

- Suicide attempts.
  For every five who complete suicide, four have made one or more previous attempts. Often these attempts are desperate cries for help by people who feel so isolated they can express their pain in no other way.

- Suicide threats.
  It is not true that those who threaten suicide don't do it, nor that they always leave a suicide note. Only 15% of suicides leave one.

- Great change in eating or sleeping habits.
- Sudden loss of interest in prized possessions.
- Dramatic change in school performance.
- Being accident-prone.
- Physical complaints.
- Withdrawal.
- Apathy, anxiety.
- Overwhelming guilt or self-hate.
- Alcohol or drug abuse.
- Promiscuous sexual activity.
- Deep and prolonged grief over any loss.
- Apparent improvement after a period of depression.
  The person is seriously vulnerable to reversal now, and has more energy to act on suicidal thoughts.

The Samaritans, *Depression, Suicide, and the College Student,* 1982.

The next psychosocial stage, intimacy versus isolation, occurs as the adolescent moves into young adulthood. In this stage the young person must deal with the issue of establishing an adult, sharing, nonexploitive relationship with another person. The young person who emerges from adolescence with a strong sense of personal identity is well prepared to establish a meaningful, loving, trusting, intimate relationship with another person. The young person who is still struggling with the issue of identity will be unable to establish a truly intimate relationship with another person and will be likely to retreat into self-absorption. These individuals tend to become increasingly isolated and unconnected as they grow older. . . .

While the behavioral perspective does not include specific age-related stages of development, the principle of modeling does have special significance for adolescence. Imitation and modeling are prevalent behaviors among this age group. Adolescents are especially likely to copy the dress, speech, mannerisms, and other behavior of their peers and of popular public figures such as rock stars. They are also more vulnerable to cluster suicides, a phenomenon in which a group of people who are similar demographically and live in the same general geographic location will commit suicide over a relatively short time span. Adolescents are vulnerable also to the "copy cat" suicide phenomenon, in which several suicides of a similar nature will occur following a single highly publicized suicide. Both of these phenomena can be understood as examples of modeling.

Searching for Meaning and Purpose

The humanistic perspective, like the behavioral perspective, does not specify stages of development. This perspective does, however, maintain that human beings are growth oriented and are continuously in the process of seeking meaning and purpose in life. The search for meaning and purpose is especially prominent during the adolescent and young adult years. Young people are heavily involved in preparation for their adult lives and in setting goals and establishing a dream for lifetime accomplishments. Because of youth's heavy orientation toward the future, the existential claim that "the future determines the present" is likely to be more true for this age group than for any other. Young people who for any reason are unable to establish and work toward important lifetime goals are likely to develop feelings of uselessness, hopelessness, and depression. . . .

Formal Thinking

According to cognitive development theory, the adolescent and young adult are in the formal operations stage. This stage is marked by the development of hypothetical and abstract thinking capabilities as well as by the intuitive use of the scientific method in problem solving. Jean Piaget believed that young people's ability to form hypotheses is particularly relevant in explaining certain characteristics of adolescent thinking. Adolescents, for the first time in their lives, are capable of dreaming of idealized worlds which do not exist. Because, however, their development has not yet progressed to a level where they can impose reality constraints upon their hypothetical "better" worlds, they are often disappointed with life as it really is. This type of thinking among adolescents may result in considerable disillusionment and unhappiness with the world and may also lead to the consideration of other hypothetical possibilities, one of which is death.

In summary, the adolescent years tend to be characterized by rapid physical growth and major psychological changes. Adolescents must cope not only with a rapidly changing physical body but also with hormonal changes that promote adult sexual responses and with cognitive changes that permit more abstract and hypothetical analyses. In addition, adolescents become more influenced by the behavior and attitudes of their peer group even as they strive to develop their own personal identity. The stress resulting from such major life changes undoubtedly taxes the adolescent's coping skills and contributes to the rates of suicide and attempted suicide among individuals aged 15-24.

"The presence of firearms in the home is a substantial risk factor for youthful suicide."

Guns in the Home Cause Teen Suicide

David A. Brent et al.

Child psychiatrist David A. Brent and a panel of colleagues completed a study that relates teen suicide to the presence of guns in the home. In the following viewpoint extracted from the study, the authors conclude that firearms substantially increase the chances of a troubled adolescent taking his or her own life. The panel contends that gun safety measures in the home are not effective in deterring youths from committing suicide, and consequently proposes that guns be removed from the homes of suicidal teenagers. Brent, associate professor at the University of Pittsburgh, is recognized for his research on at-risk youth.

As you read, consider the following questions:

1. What are the three sample groups the panel uses to study?
2. Which sample group had the most guns per household, according to the authors?
3. What suggestions does the panel give that society and physicians can take to decrease teen suicide by guns?

Excerpted, with permission, from "The Presence and Accessibility of Firearms in the Homes of Adolescent Suicides: A Case Control Study," by David A. Brent et al., *Journal of the American Medical Association* 226:21 (December 4, 1991), pp. 2989-2995, © 1991, American Medical Association.

The doubling in the adolescent suicide rate over the past three decades is largely accounted for by an increase in firearms suicides. This has led to the hypothesis that the increase in the adolescent suicide rate may, in part, be explained by an increased availability of firearms to adolescents. Some investigators have cautiously concluded that restriction in the availability of firearms might result in a reduction in the adolescent suicide rate. . . .

Significant Risk

A report suggests that more restrictive gun control laws, while not of any significant benefit to older persons with respect to suicide, are associated with a reduced suicide rate among adolescents and young adults aged 15 to 24 years. The suicide rates of two similar cities, Vancouver, British Columbia, and Seattle, Wash., were compared. Adolescents and young adults aged 15 to 24 years in Seattle had a suicide rate 1.4 times higher than that of their Vancouver counterparts, a difference accounted for by a 10-fold elevation in the firearms suicide rate among the Seattle youths. This difference in the adolescent and young adult suicide rate was thought to be attributable to less restrictive gun control laws and to the greater availability of firearms in Seattle.

Although this study clearly implicates the importance of the availability of firearms in youthful suicide, it is unknown what role the availability of firearms played in each individual suicide, because of the ecological nature of the design. However, other work suggests that the presence of a gun in the home is much more likely to result in a suicide than in a defensible homicide. Additionally, we have previously reported the results of a case-control study comparing adolescent suicide victims with suicidal psychiatric inpatients with respect to the availability of firearms in their homes. Suicide completers were 2.5 times more likely to have a gun in their home than were diagnostically similar, psychiatrically ill, suicidal adolescents, thus suggesting that the availability of firearms represents a significant risk factor for adolescent suicide. . . .

In the present study, we addressed the following hypotheses: (1) guns will be found more frequently in the homes of suicide victims than in the homes of the control groups, (2) handguns will be more closely associated with suicide than long guns, (3) guns will be stored in a more easily accessible manner in the homes of suicide victims, and (4) guns will be associated with suicide independent of demographic or psychiatric characteristics.

The suicide completer sample was a consecutive series of suicide victims aged 19 years and younger drawn from 28 Western Pennsylvania counties over a period from July 1986 through February 1988. Of 64 adolescent suicides that occurred over this

time, the families of 48 youthful victims agreed to participate. . . .

The suicide attempter sample was drawn from the adolescent
inpatient units at Western Psychiatric Institute and Clinic
(WPIC), a state-affiliated university hospital that draws from a
large geographic area and provides treatment for patients repre-
senting the full socioeconomic spectrum. Of 97 attempters approached for participation, 90 agreed to participate. . . .

Misguided, Impulsive Acts

Results of research on risk factors and patterns of suicide suggest
that adolescent suicide may be a very different phenomenon than
suicide among adults, particularly the elderly. Elderly people
who commit suicide seem to be more likely to have a clear and
sustained intent to do so. Young people, on the other hand, are
impulsive and not particularly skilled in communication. For
them, a suicide attempt may be an attempt to communicate that
they are in great pain, although they may be ambivalent about
wanting to die. For such adolescents, ready access to a firearm
may guarantee that their plea for help will not be heard. Access
to a firearm may not make them violent, but it can make their
self-directed violence fatal and very final.

Mark L. Rosenberg, James A. Mercy, Vernon N. Houk, *The Journal of the American
Medical Association*, December 4, 1991.

The never-suicidal psychiatric patient group (referred to in this
report as psychiatric controls) was drawn from the same inpatient units at WPIC as noted above, with similar inclusionary
and exclusionary criteria, except that the psychiatric controls
could not have had current or past clinically significant suicidality (suicidal ideation with a plan or intent, or actual suicidal behavior). Of 116 patients who were approached, 103 consented to
participate. . . .

The total sample of 90 attempters and 103 psychiatric controls
differed from the completers on age, gender, and county of origin. Therefore, 47 attempters and 47 psychiatric controls were
selected on these three variables and were frequency matched
to the sample of suicide victims, so that there were no statistically significant differences among the three groups on the
above-noted demographic factors. . . .

Firearms in the Home

The majority of suicide victims killed themselves with a gun
(69%), whereas none of the suicide attempters used a gun in
their attempt. The majority of suicide victims with a gun in

their home died of a firearms suicide, whereas suicide by firearms was infrequent in those suicide victims without a gun in the house. Firearms were more frequently present in the homes of suicide victims compared with both attempters and psychiatric controls.

The mean number of guns per household for completers was significantly greater than for attempters or for psychiatric controls. Completers had significantly greater numbers of both long guns and handguns in their homes than did either attempters or psychiatric controls.

Type of Gun

Relative to both control groups, suicide victims were more likely to have both long guns and handguns in their homes. Suicide victims who had both handguns and long guns present in the home were slightly more likely to make use of the handgun than the long gun. However, of the eight suicide victims who only had long guns available to them, six used these weapons to kill themselves. . . .

The majority of suicide victims who had guns in their home used them, regardless of whether the guns were stored locked (three of five used firearms), separate from ammunition, together with ammunition, or loaded (four of four). The methods of storage of firearms among the three groups were examined to see if firearms were more readily accessible in the homes of completers than in those of the two inpatient control groups. Given the presence of at least one gun in the household, there was no difference in method of storage of firearms among the three groups. . . . However, there were nonstatistically significant trends in the direction of a greater proportion of completers storing guns loaded or together with ammunition than either attempters or psychiatric controls.

Various Factors

The availability of firearms (both all guns and handguns) in the home was compared between suicides and the two inpatient control groups after stratification on each of the following variables: gender, county of origin, the presence of a man in the home, history of inpatient treatment, and psychiatric disorder. The availability of firearms was greater in the homes of completers than in the homes of either of the two control groups, regardless of stratification variables. . . . Therefore, the greater availability of firearms in the homes of suicide victims compared with inpatient controls was a consistent finding, independent of gender, county of origin, the presence of a man in the home, inpatient treatment history, or psychiatric diagnosis. . . .

In this report, we have replicated our previous findings that suicide completers are more likely to have a gun in their home than a diagnostically comparable group of psychiatric inpatients. We have established that these findings apply for comparisons of completers with both suicide attempters and a group of never-suicidal psychiatric controls and have demonstrated that these differences are independent of demographic variables, history of inpatient treatment, or psychiatric diagnoses. As in our previous work, the physical presence of firearms in the home appears to be a much more significant contributor to suicidal risk than does the type of gun available or the manner in which the firearms were stored. . . .

Standard of Practice

Physicians should routinely ask all adolescents at risk for suicide whether they have access to a gun. They should also ask the parents whether a gun is in the house, and when the answer is yes, they should work with the parents to get it out of the house. Asking about access to guns should be a routine part of taking a medical history from an adolescent at risk and should be taught in medical schools, written about in textbooks, and made part of every history-taking protocol. Today, the question of whether an adolescent at risk of committing suicide has access to a gun is all but ignored. It should become the standard of practice.

Mark L. Rosenberg, James A. Mercy, Vernon N. Houk, *The Journal of the American Medical Association*, December 4, 1991.

While some may hope for an achievement in the reduction in the firearms suicide rate by more restrictive gun control laws, others predict that this potential reduction will be offset by an increase in the suicide rate due to other means. However, method substitution may be less likely to occur in adolescents and young adults, possibly because of the prominent role that impulsivity and substance abuse play in youthful suicide. The availability of a gun may play a more critical role in determining the lethality of a suicide attempt among impulsive youth than in older adults for whom suicide is a more premeditated act.

Handguns Versus Long Guns

Suicide victims who had access to either a handgun or a long gun were slightly (and nonsignificantly) more likely to choose a handgun. However, victims who had access to only one type of weapon were both equally and highly likely to resort to suicide by firearms. Therefore, the availability of both handguns and long guns should be considered a risk factor for adolescent suicide. One cautionary note should be introduced about the potential benefits of stricter handgun control. Although decreasing the availability of handguns may well have a beneficial effect on the youthful suicide rate, nearly half of the firearms suicides in this series were attributable to long guns.

Firearms-Free Homes

In this study, we showed that firearms in the homes of suicide victims were stored in a manner no more easily accessible than were guns in the homes of the control subjects. . . . However, the effect of accessibility remains small in comparison to that of physical presence, and, in fact, three of five victims in whose homes firearms were stored locked killed themselves with that gun. Good gun safety habits are not likely to be protective against suicide, insofar as firearms in the home are probably a risk factor for adolescent suicide regardless of the manner of storage. Therefore, all guns must be removed from the home of an adolescent assessed to be at risk for suicide. . . .

Legislation that enforces a 1- or 2-week waiting period before the purchase of a weapon, however beneficial for other reasons, is unlikely to have an impact on the adolescent suicide rate. None of the firearms suicides in this series were incurred by weapons obtained for the purpose of suicide within 1 or 2 weeks prior to death. Instead, adolescent suicides may be prevented by increasing the proportion of firearms-free homes, whether through legislation similar to Canada's, or through a campaign of public education about the hazards of firearms ownership.

Substantial Risk

The above-noted findings, taken in context with the extant literature, strongly indicate that the presence of firearms in the home is a substantial risk factor for youthful suicide, especially in those already at risk for psychiatric reasons. The general controversy regarding gun licensure and ownership notwithstanding, it is clear that firearms have no place in the homes of psychiatrically troubled adolescents. Inquiry about the presence and method of storage of firearms in the homes of young patients should become a routine part of general pediatric and psychiatric care. Physicians who care for psychiatrically disturbed adolescents with any indicators of suicidal risk, such as depression, conduct problems, substance abuse, or suicidal thoughts, have a responsibility to make a clear and firm recommendation that firearms be removed from the homes of these at-risk youth.

"Abuse of substances is a potentially important risk factor in suicidal behavior early in life."

Alcohol and Drug Abuse Causes Teen Suicide

Marc A. and Judith J. Schuckit

In the following viewpoint, Marc A. and Judith J. Schuckit conclude that suicidal adolescents are prone to commit suicide under the influence of alcohol or drugs. These adolescents, the authors find, use chemical substances both to commit suicide and to give themselves courage to commit the act. Marc A. Schuckit, professor of psychiatry at the University of California Medical School, is the director of the Alcohol Research Center, San Diego Veterans Administration Medical Center, San Diego, California. Judith J. Schuckit is a former research assistant.

As you read, consider the following questions:

1. In the authors' opinion, in what specific ways do alcohol and drug abuse cause teen suicide?
2. According to the Schuckits, what ways do parents contribute to suicidal behavior in their adolescent children?
3. How can substance abuse indirectly lead to teen suicide, according to the authors?

Adapted from the Alcohol, Drug Abuse, and Mental Health Administration's *Report of the Secretary's Task Force on Youth Suicide, vol. 2: Risk Factors for Youth Suicide* by Marc A. and Judith J. Schuckit. Washington, DC: U.S. Government Printing Office, 1989.

About 10 percent or more of people in the general population reported suicidal feelings over the prior year, including 2.5 percent who had more intense thoughts. Counting all age groups, actual suicide attempts are observed at a rate between 100 and 800/100,000/yr, with women age 15 to 24 years standing out. . . . In men, the 15 to 24 year olds also predominate, but in each age group the actual rates are about half those seen in women.

Attempts

Since the peak age for suicide attempts is between 15 and 24 years old, it is not surprising that a number of studies have focused specifically on the attempt rate for children and adolescents. Looking first at more anecdotal data on children who have sought help, it has been estimated that 3 percent of a consecutive series of young people coming to private practice or psychiatric outpatient settings had ever attempted suicide. The same is true for 10 percent to 30 percent of adolescents coming to emergency rooms, and the rate of attempts increases to between 10 percent and 50 percent among young psychiatric inpatients. These figures are probably inflated because of the troubled nature of the populations observed.

The high prevalence of suicide attempts in any age group, including adolescents, is not a new phenomenon. Most of the literature focuses on more anecdotal reports; between 1972 and 1980 there was a five-fold increase in adolescents seen for suicide attempts in a Louisville, Kentucky psychiatric hospital, and an almost doubling of adolescent suicidal behavior was seen between 1970 and 1975 in a New Haven, Connecticut emergency room.

Suicide Completions

Suicide completion is a much rarer phenomenon than suicide attempt. The ratio between the two depends upon the definitions used, but is at least 10 to 1, and could be as high as 100 or more to 1 in some groups. There is, however, an important connection between attempts and completions, because as many as 50 percent or more of completers have attempted suicide in the past. . . .

As infrequent as completed suicide is in the general population, it is even less common among adolescents. However, self-inflicted death has long rated as the third leading cause of mortality in this otherwise healthy group, especially for youth with histories of psychiatric care. Despite isolated cases of apparent short-term "epidemics" of suicidal behavior among young people, completed suicide is especially rare for children under age 15.

The prevalence of suicides in the United States and Canada

appears to have been stable during the 1950s. However, as reported for attempts, suicidal death began to increase in the 1960s. The overall rate in 1961 was 5/100,000/yr for men and 1 for women in Alberta, Canada; almost double the figures from 1951. Self-inflicted death rose to 25 and 5 for the two sexes by 1971, on to approximately 32 and 5 by 1972. In general, the U.S. suicide rate rose from 5.2 to 13.3/100,000/yr from 1960 to 1980. Other investigators have also documented an increase of at least two- to three-fold between 1960 and 1980.

Direct Association

Alcohol and drug use and violent death (accidents, homicide, and suicide) are potentially related in a number of ways. Drugs of abuse, especially brain depressants (e.g. barbiturates, antianxiety drugs, and alcohol) and brain stimulants (e.g. amphetamines, cocaine, weight reducing products) can impair judgment, increase levels of impulsivity, and are capable of producing severe mood disturbances, including temporary, intense and suicidal depressions. . . .

Causes of Death for Ages 15-24

Suicide now ranks as the third leading cause of death among people ages 15 to 24. Some deaths classified as highway accidents may actually be suicides.

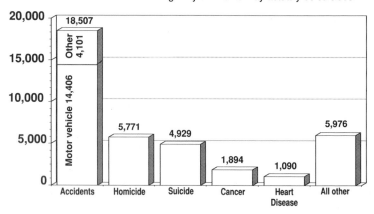

Source: Department of Health and Human Services, National Center for Health Statistics, 1988.

One obvious association between substances and suicide is the use of alcohol or drugs as vehicles for the suicidal act. Historically, drug overdoses of prescription or over-the-counter drugs have been a favored mechanism in suicide attempts, especially overdoses with brain depressants in women. The use of drugs as the mechanism of attempt by young people is equally strong. In one consecutive series of 505 adolescents and children seen in a pediatric emergency room for a suicide attempt, 88 percent had used drug overdose, as had 78 percent to 100 percent of suicide attempting youth reported in other samples, although some authors have reported lower rates. . . .

Drugs and Suicide

Analyses of data for adolescents also document a close association between substances and suicide. This conclusion is supported by studies of suicidal youth, evaluations of substance abusers, and through observation of young psychiatric patients.

Adolescents who fulfill criteria for drug abuse or who have relatively heavy drug intake patterns have an increased rate of death overall, including high rates of suicide. A 10-year followup of two groups of teenagers (one from the general population and the second identified because of prior drug use) revealed a two- to seven-fold increased death rate among boys with histories of drug misuse, and an almost two-fold to eightfold increased death rate among girls. Approximately half of this increase in death rate was from suicide.

The relationship between drugs, alcohol, and suicide in young people is corroborated when populations identified because of suicidal behavior are evaluated. A. Patel reported that among suicide attempters age 12 to 19 years old, 41 percent of the boys and 19 percent of the girls had been drinking immediately before the attempt, and B. Garfinkel found a ten-fold higher rate of recent alcohol or drug use in 505 adolescent attempters than for controls. M. Shafii noted "frequent use of nonprescription drugs or alcohol" among 70 percent of the 20 teenagers who committed suicide in the Louisville area between 1980 and 1983, while almost half of the suicides aged 15 to 19 in Erie County, New York, had alcohol in their blood. The study of suicides under age 30 in San Diego found that more than 75 percent abused drugs or alcohol, including between a third and a half for whom these diagnoses were the primary illnesses. Among those with drug problems in the San Diego sample, 79 percent had abused marijuana, 45 percent cocaine, 34 percent amphetamines, and about 25 percent each had abused opiates, sedatives/hypnotics, or hallucinogens. There was an average of three to five substances abused per individual.

Added Medical Seriousness

The association between suicidal behavior and drugs is just as strong among adolescent psychiatric patients. D. Robbins and N. Alessi studied 33 teenage psychiatric inpatients who had histories of prior suicide attempts, looking for the relationship between alcohol or drug use and suicidal behavior. They used an analysis of correlation that evaluates the degree to which two factors change at the same time (the higher the correlation, the greater the similarity in change). A history of alcohol abuse correlated with the number of past suicidal "gestures" at a 0.42 level, accounting for 25 percent of the variance or range of the number of gestures in this group. Similarly, the correlation between alcohol abuse and the seriousness of past attempts was 0.35, and alcohol problems correlated with the level of medical seriousness at 0.36. Overall, the association between a history of alcohol abuse and the occurrence of a suicide attempt was 0.28. A history of drug abuse correlated with the number of suicide "gestures" at 0.32, and with the medical seriousness at 0.26. Those authors conclude that "substance abuse in depressed adolescents appears both to increase the risk of multiple attempts and to add to the medical seriousness of the attempt.". . .

Linking Suicide and Substance Abuse in Youth

Among heavy substance users:	Four fold increased suicidal death rate
Among adolescent suicide attempters:	Ten fold increased substance use
	30 percent drank before attempt
Among adolescent suicide completers:	70 percent used drugs frequently
	50 percent had alcohol in blood
	75 percent fit criteria for drug or alcohol use disorders
Among young psychiatric patients:	Suicidal behavior and substance abuse correlate

---

Alcoholism or other illness in parents are relatively common findings among suicidal children and teenagers. It is possible that substance abuse or psychiatric disorders in these parents might have contributed to the increased rate of broken homes and chaotic childhood lifestyles for young people; these children may have a high risk for early onset of the disorder itself. Therefore, the suicidal behavior in these children may sometimes reflect their own early onset of illness associated with disordered mood or judgment.

In summary, substance abuse or psychiatric disorders in parents could contribute to the suicidal behavior in young people in at least two ways. First, some of the self-destructive problems in these children could have been influenced by the models set by the rearing parents, as well as the child's reaction to the anger and frustration engendered by the behavior of the ill parent. Second, some of the suicidal behavior observed in the children may reflect the inheritance of a predisposition towards the genetically influenced illness itself, with concomitant suicidal risk associated with the disorder and not just the specific childhood environment. . . .

Whether studied in the general population or among groups in treatment, substance abusing young people have a significantly increased rate of self-inflicted death; youth identified because of their suicidal behavior frequently use and abuse nonprescription drugs and alcohol; and there is a close relationship between substance misuse patterns and the number and severity of suicide attempts.

Indirect Associations

Suicidal behavior early in life is also associated with substance problems in more indirect ways. Diagnoses such as the ASPD (antisocial personality disorder) and "borderline personality" carry high risks for both self-harm and substance misuse. It is also probable that heavy drinking or drug use during major depressive episodes or in the midst of other psychiatric problems can exacerbate problems and might contribute to a suicide attempt or completion in these high risk individuals. A third indirect association between substance abuse and self-harm relates to the probable importance of genetic factors in the development of alcoholism and early onset psychiatric disorders. Thus, for example, children of alcoholics are more likely than the general population to observe suicidal behavior in their parents, more likely to suffer chaotic homes during childhood, and themselves have a genetically increased risk for both suicidal behavior and substance misuse.

From this review it is appropriate to conclude that, through both direct and indirect mechanisms, intake and abuse of substances is a potentially important risk factor in suicidal behavior early in life.

"Society influences suicidal behavior by gay and lesbian youth [through] the ongoing discrimination against . . . homosexuals. "

Society's Rejection of Homosexual Teens Causes Suicide

Paul Gibson

In the following viewpoint, Paul Gibson states that homosexual teenagers are three times more likely to commit suicide than heterosexuals. He states that society stigmatizes and discriminates against gay and lesbian teenagers, leading them to feelings of despair and sometimes suicide. Gibson is a licensed clinical social worker who works as a therapist and program consultant in San Francisco, California.

As you read, consider the following questions:

1. According to Gibson, how does society influence suicidal behavior in gay and lesbian youth?
2. What is the most significant factor in youth suicide, according to the author?
3. In Gibson's opinion, why do most gay and lesbian youth have a negative picture of their future adult life?

Adapted from the Alcohol, Drug Abuse, and Mental Health Administration's *Report of the Secretary's Task Force on Youth Suicide, vol. 3: Prevention and Intervention in Youth Suicide* by Paul Gibson. Washington, DC: U.S. Government Printing Office, 1989.

Suicide is the leading cause of death among gay male, lesbian, bisexual and transsexual youth. They are part of two populations at serious risk of suicide: sexual minorities and the young. Agency statistics and coroner reports seldom reflect how suicidal behavior is related to sexual orientation or identity issues. The literature on youth suicide has virtually ignored the subject. Research in recent years, however, with homosexual young people and adults has revealed a serious problem with cause for alarm. . . .

Overwhelming Pressure

Gay young people face the same risk factors for suicidal behavior that affect other youth. These include family problems, breaking up with a lover, social isolation, school failure, and identity conflicts. However, these factors assume greater importance when the youth has a gay or lesbian orientation. K. Jay and A. Young found that 53 percent of gay males and 33 percent of lesbians surveyed believed their suicide attempts involved their homosexuality. A. Bell and M. Weinberg report that 58 percent of gay males and 39 percent of lesbians felt their first suicide attempts were related to the fact that they were homosexuals. Suicide attempts by gay and lesbian youth are even more likely to involve conflicts around their sexual orientation because of the overwhelming pressures they face in coming out at an early age. . . .

It is a sobering fact to realize that we are the greatest risk factors in gay youth suicide. No group of people are more strongly affected by the attitudes and conduct of society than are the young. Gay and lesbian youth are strongly affected by the negative attitudes and hostile responses of society to homosexuality. The resulting poor self-esteem, depression, and fear can be a fatal blow to a fragile identity. Two ways that society influences suicidal behavior by gay and lesbian youth are: 1) the ongoing discrimination against and oppression of homosexuals, and 2) the portrayal of homosexuals as being self-destructive.

It is the response of our society as a whole to homosexuality, and specifically those institutions and significant others responsible for their care, that pose the greatest risk to gay and lesbian youth. T. Gock believes that homophobia, the irrational fear and hatred of homosexuals, is the root of the problem. Gay males and lesbians are still routinely the victims of violence by others. In a survey of nearly 2,100 lesbians and gay men nationwide, the National Gay Task Force found that more than 90 percent had been victims of verbal and physical assault because of their sexual orientation. Tacit and explicit discrimination against homosexuals is still pervasive in virtually all areas of life. Half of the States still prohibit homosexual relationships between con-senting adults. Homosexuals are not allowed to legally marry and form "legitimate" long-term relationships. The vast majority of States and municipalities still discriminate against lesbians and gay men in housing, employment, and others areas. Gay and lesbian youth see this and take it to heart. . . .

Gay and Lesbian Youth in Suicide Crisis

Mark Wood, a gay teenager from Seattle, Wash., committed suicide after he got an honorable discharge from the Marines. After talking to his minister, the 18-year-old went into the chapel, knelt at the altar, and shot himself.

Gay and lesbian teenagers are killing themselves in staggering numbers. They are hanging themselves in high school classrooms, jumping from bridges, shooting themselves on church altars, cutting themselves with razor blades, and downing lethal numbers of pills.

A conservatively estimated 1,500 young gay and lesbian lives are terminated every year because these troubled youths have nowhere to turn. They are scared and alone.

Shira Maguen, *The Advocate*, September 24, 1991.

E. Rofes maintains we have created a stereotyped image of the unhappy homosexual in literature and the media for which suicide is the only appropriate resolution. This image is reinforced by the fact that homosexual characters in novels and films invariably kill themselves in the end. The myth is perpetuated by the absence of positive adult gay role models in our society where, historically, the only known homosexuals were those exposed by scandal and disgraced in their communities. Rofes maintains this creates a strong negative context for the early identity formation of young gay males and lesbians effectively socializing them into suicidal feelings and behavior. He sees a strong correlation between sexual orientation, social response to that sexual orientation, and subsequent suicidality in an individual.

A predisposing factor in suicidal feelings among many adolescents is poor self-esteem. This is especially true for gay adolescents who have internalized a harshly negative image of being bad and wrong from society, religion, family, and peers. For youth, a poor self-image contributes substantially to a lack of confidence in being able to cope with problems. The images of homosexuals as sick and self-destructive have impact on the coping skills of gay youth, rendering them helpless and unable to improve their situation. Gay youth who have internalized a message throughout their lives of being worthless and unable to cope from abusive and chaotic families are at even greater risk. . . .

Many youth realize they are gay or lesbian but attempt to hide their orientation from others. They suffer from chronic loneliness and depression. They may attempt suicide because they feel trapped in their situation and believe they do not deserve to live. A suicidal gesture may be a cry for help from these youth for others to recognize and understand their situation. Finally, those youth who are open about being gay, lesbian, or bisexual face continuous conflict with their environment. They remain vulnerable to suicide because they face these extreme pressures with a more fragile sense of self-worth and ability to cope with life than other youth.

Family and Religion

Family problems are probably the most significant factor in youth suicide. Youth derive their core sense of being cared about and belonging from their families. Gay youth may make suicide attempts after being rejected by their families. For gay and lesbian youth forced to leave home, the loss of parental love and support remains a critical issue for them. Sometimes the youth's sexual orientation becomes a convenient excuse for parents to reject a son or daughter they did not want. Youth from abusive and dysfunctional families are at even greater risk. K. Wandrei found, in comparing suicide attempts by lesbians and heterosexual women, that lesbians were more likely to come from broken homes. . . .

Gay and lesbian youth may feel suicidal because of a failure to meet family expectations. All youth need approval from their parents. Some youth report only feeling loved by parents when they are fulfilling their parents' image of who they should be. Gay youth often feel they can not meet their parents' standards and may attempt suicide after real or anticipated disappointment by their families that they will not fit the social script of heterosexual marriage and grandchildren. This pressure is particularly strong for lesbians. Gay youth fear they will not have families of their own and be alone as adults with no one to care for them. . . .

Religion presents another risk factor in gay youth suicide because of the depiction of homosexuality as a sin and the reliance of families on the church for understanding homosexuality. Many traditional (e.g., Catholicism) and fundamentalist (e.g., Baptist) faiths still portray homosexuality as morally wrong or evil. Family religious beliefs can be a primary reason for parents forcing youth to leave home if a homosexual orientation is seen as incompatible with church teachings. These beliefs can also create unresolvable internal conflicts for gay youth who adhere to their faith but believe they will not change their sexual orientation. They may feel wicked and condemned to hell and attempt suicide in despair of ever obtaining redemption. . . .

The failure of schools to educate youth about homosexuality presents another risk factor to gay and lesbian adolescents. By ignoring the subject in all curricula, including family life classes, the schools deny access to positive information about homosexuality that could improve the self-esteem of gay youth. They also perpetuate myths and stereotypes that condemn homosexuality and deny youth access to positive adult lesbian and gay role models. This silence provides tacit support for homophobic attitudes and conduct by some students.

Social Isolation and Substance Abuse

Social isolation has been consistently identified as one of the most critical factors in suicide attempts by youth. The isolation and alienation young people experience in all aspects of their lives can be overwhelming. Those youth hiding their identity often withdraw from family and friends out of fear of being discovered. They feel there is no one they can talk to and no one who will understand. . . .

Openly gay youth experience blatant rejection and isolation from others. One young gay male related that his parents refuse to eat at the dinner table with him after they learned he was gay. Male peers cruelly separate themselves from young gay males with jokes about not wanting to get AIDS. Gay youth frequently do not have contact with other gay adolescents or adults for support. Parents often forbid them from associating with people they "suspect" or know to be homosexuals. Youth service workers often feel uncomfortable talking with gay young people because of their prejudices and lack of understanding for who they are. The Los Angeles Suicide Prevention Center, in their recent study on gay youth suicide, ironically found that gay young people rated social support as being very important to them while simultaneously experiencing people as being more rejecting of them than did other youth.

Some gay and lesbian young people cope with the many problems they face by using alcohol and drugs. The age of onset for substance use among all youth has become lower in recent years and in 1985 is estimated to be 11.9 years for boys and 12.7 years for girls. This coincides with the age that many youth are becoming aware of a gay or lesbian orientation. Rofes found that lesbians and gay men have a higher rate of substance abuse than heterosexuals and found this to be correlated with increased suicidal feelings and behavior. . . .

Gay youth forced to live on the streets experience more severe drug problems. The Larkin Street Youth Center in San Francisco reported that more than 75 percent of their clients identified as gay had serious and chronic disorders. The Los Angeles Suicide Prevention Center found a strong correlation between substance abuse and suicide attempts among gay young people.

Professional Help

Perhaps no risk factor is as insidious or unique to the suicidal behavior of gay and lesbian youth than receiving professional help. The large number of gay youth who have had contact with mental health and social work services during their turbulent adolescent years would seem to be a positive indicator for improving their stability and future outlook. This is sadly not often the case. Many helping professionals still refuse to recognize or accept a homosexual orientation in youth despite growing evidence that sexual orientation is formed by adolescence. They refuse to support a homosexual orientation in youth despite the fact that homosexuality is no longer viewed as a mental disorder. . . .

Facing a Hostile World

About 30% of the 1 million attempted teen suicides each year are committed by gays or lesbians.

"Society's ingrained prejudices against gay people are literally killing staggering numbers," said David LaFontaine, lobbying director for the Coalition for Lesbian and Gay Civil Rights. "They are trapped in an environment that is overwhelmingly hostile."

New York Native, December 2, 1991.

Youth who are aware of their lesbian or gay orientation but hide it from others, may seek help without identifying their concerns about their sexuality. We often do not recognize these youth because we don't acknowledge they exist. We are uncomfortable in discussing or addressing the issue and consequently are unable to identify or resolve the source of the youth's conflicts. A suicide attempt may be an effort by the youth to force the issue and bring it to our attention. It may also be an act of despair over a problem that they feel can not be addressed through professional help.

Even openly gay and lesbian youth are subjected to treatment with potentially adverse effects. Frequently, informing family and counselors that a youth is gay is the impetus for imposed treatment. We assume that the youth's gay orientation is the source of the problem rather than the response of others to his/her being lesbian or gay. Encouraging these youth to change can cause regression in the development of a healthy gay identity and reinforce traditional stereotypes of homosexuals as sick and self-destructive. This, in turn, further weakens the youth's self-esteem and ability to cope with problems. Even those professionals who accept the youth as gay or lesbian are often unable to support the youngster in dealing with conflicts at home and in school. . . .

Group home placements present special hardships for gay youth because abusive peers often live in the same home with them. Those programs without an on-site school require gay youth to return to public school for their education. Program staff have seldom received training on issues and concerns related to homosexuality. They are frequently unable to understand or work with gay youth effectively. Group homes become a living hell of harassment, isolation, and conflicts with other staff and residents offering gay youth little support and no resolution. A suicide attempt may be an effort to force removal from the placement and find a different home. Many homes, however, will not accept gay youth and few offer specialized services to meet their needs. . . .

Romantic Attachments

Intimate relationships are the primary focus of hostility and discrimination against homosexuals. Society severely restricts where homosexuals can meet, prevents public displays of affection between them, and does not allow legal marriages to be formed. Gay and lesbian youth suffer greater isolation than homosexual adults and far greater social deprivation than other adolescents. It is extremely difficult for them to meet other homosexuals and they frequently do not know anyone like themselves. Gay youth who hide their identity often form their first romantic attachments to unknowing friends, teachers, and peers. These are often cases of unrequited love with the youth never revealing their true feelings. Gay youth are fragile in these situations and may experience despair or suicidal feelings from never being able to fulfill their hopes for a relationship. Some gay youth bravely reveal their feelings and may attempt suicide after blatant rejection by a teacher or the loss of a close friend. . . .

Independent Living

Gay and lesbian youth are more likely than other adolescents to be forced to leave home and become self-sufficient prematurely. Some of these youth have been hiding their identities and can no longer stand the extreme isolation in their lives. Many others have been rejected by families and have dropped out of school, effectively forced out of their communities because of their sexual orientation. . . .

Gay youth living on the streets are at greater risk of suicide due to repeated exposure to chronic substance abuse, physical and sexual assault, and sexually transmitted diseases including AIDS. Their contact with the limited segment of gay adults involved in street life confirms a negative image of homosexuality and they remain unaware of the variety of positive adult gay lifestyles open to them. Their relationships are tenuous and complicated by dependence on their lovers for support. Some gay and lesbian youth engage in increasingly reckless and self-destructive behavior as an expression of the sadness and anger they feel because of the unresolved issues with their families and despair over their new life. A suicide attempt may result from a negative contact with their family, breaking up with a lover, or failure to make it on their own. . . .

AIDS

The attitudes of young gay males towards exposure to AIDS ranges from denial to extreme fear to not caring. One young male said he was not concerned because "teenagers do not get AIDS." Another was convinced that a head cold he had developed was the first symptom of AIDS. Those who are at greatest risk may be those who simply do not care whether they are exposed to the virus. Some gay youth have an uncaring approach to life that reflects a "suicidal script." They are more prone to self-destructive behavior because of the severity of the problems they have experienced throughout their lives and specifically in relation to their sexual orientation. Contracting AIDS becomes for them the fulfillment of a life of pain and suffering they no longer want to cope with. They feel that they deserve to die.

A final risk factor for gay and lesbian youth suicide is a bleak outlook for the future. Young people have difficulty seeing a future life that is different from the present. Gay and lesbian youth fear their lives will always be as unhappy and hard as they presently are. They do not know that they will receive any more caring, acceptance, and support than they are getting now. The little information they have about homosexuality usually reinforces these mistaken beliefs. Gay youth do not understand what life could be like as a gay male or lesbian adult. They do not have accurate information about homosexuality, positive role models to pattern themselves after, or knowledge of gay and lesbian adult lifestyles and communities. Lesbian and gay youth frequently don't know that many lesbian and gay male adults lead stable, happy, and productive lives. They go through adolescence feeling lonely, afraid, and hopeless. Sometimes they take their own lives.

"Religion and the family are . . . the solution to the youth suicide problem."

The Decline of Religion and Family Causes Teen Suicide

Allan C. Carlson

In the following viewpoint, Allan C. Carlson states that the breakdown of the family and the loss of religious values have led to an increase in teen suicide. The increase in divorce and decrease in religious involvement have caused teenagers to feel alienated and have led some to commit suicide, Carlson argues. He contends that religious groups, and not government action, will help restore the values necessary to prevent teenage suicide. Carlson has written extensively on family issues and is president of The Rockford Institute and publisher of the institute's newsletter *The Family in America.*

As you read, consider the following questions:

1. According to Carlson, what did Emile Durkheim believe about the value of religion?
2. What research does the author cite to substantiate his point of view?
3. According to the author, how will establishing family and religious values reduce youth suicide?

From Allan C. Carlson, *Family Questions: Reflections on the American Social Crisis.* New Brunswick, NJ: Transaction Books, 1988. Reprinted with permission.

There are few human tragedies greater than a youth taking his own life. In America, a social and political system intended to offer unprecedented opportunities and freedom to all citizens has clearly and utterly failed the suicidal adolescent. . . .

Bigger than It Appears

Contrary to popular belief, the facts behind youth suicide suggest that we do not now face a crisis, in the sense of a rapidly growing or radically changing problem. It is true that between 1960 and 1977 there was a dramatic increase in the number of youth suicides. Yet even in 1975, near the peak year, their actual number was quite small. . . .

Nonetheless, the cries for government action are rising in intensity. Why? Answers become apparent as we examine the rhetoric of the new youth suicide campaign. A common technique, for example, is to argue that the problem is far bigger than it appears. Writing in *Child Welfare*, Donald McGuire and Margot Ely state that "experts in the field" agree "that the statistics severely mask the reality": many suicides, they say, are incorrectly labeled accidents; parents conceal suicide attempts; and so on. There is, the authors add, a continuum of self-destructive impulses, leaving virtually all young persons at risk to some degree. Psychiatrist Cynthia Pfeffer plays the same game, arguing that while the suicide rate for children, ages 6-12, is low (it is well under .1 per 100,000), "suicide threats and attempts are not rare . . . and may be increasing." She points to one study at an outpatient psychiatric clinic which found 33 percent of children to have "contemplated, threatened, and/or attempted suicide." Through conjectural statistics, an almost insignificant number is elevated to a third of the population.

Other advocates of state intervention craft arguments that are surprisingly similar to those that have been used in the push for sex education. According to Charlotte Ross, director of the pacesetting San Mateo (CA) County Suicide Prevention and Crisis Center and de facto theoretician for the movement, youngsters "desperately want to know about suicide." Educators need to strip away the religious taboos surrounding youth suicide, and "replace the cloak of mystery . . . with information that offers ways for adolescents to help both themselves and each other.". . .

Mixed Messages

Youth suicide intervenors cast parents in an odd, seemingly contradictory light. On some occasions, inadequate parents are blamed for the tragedy. According to Ross, today's teenagers must go through the normal agonies of adolescence while their world is being shaken by "social tremors" such as divorce, remarriage, and "reconstituted families.". . .

On other occasions, though, action advocates go out of their way to deny that divorce, working mothers, or family problems are to blame. In her *People* magazine lament about her son Justin's suicide while she was at work, mother Anne Spoonhour emphasizes that neither she nor her husband feel any guilt about the death: "We both accept that this was his decision and not ours." In the same issue, Pamela Cantor, president-elect of the American Association of Suicidology, directly denies that divorce and working mothers are to blame: "What is important is that both parents be involved with their children, whether they are divorced or together.". . .

Principal Target

Lurking behind such disjointed logic are professionals on the make, who sense piles of government money just over the horizon. Speaking for *school counselors*, Jacquelin Greuling and Richard DeBlassie argue that they can assume the role of "true friend" towards troubled teens and so render "a unique, unmistakably gratifying and life-saving service to young people.". . .

A Lack of Support

According to psychologist Calvin Frederick, "The primary underlying cause of the rising suicide rate among American youth seems to be a breakdown in the nuclear family unit." While the disintegration of the nuclear family is an easy target—it has been blamed for everything from asthma to schizophrenia—there is evidence that at a developmental stage when they are most in need of it, adolescents have been receiving less support.

George Howe Colt, *The Enigma of Suicide*, 1991.

The schools are their principal target. As psychologist Irving Berkovitz coyly notes, public schools are the places "where the behavior and feelings of the majority of children first come to the close attention of professionally trained adults outside the nuclear family," i.e., the places where the experts get their turn at the expense of Mom and Dad. Parents are not trusted by students, Charlotte Ross argues; teenagers turn most often to their peers. She advocates school-based prevention programs for all children, training them "both as potential victims and potential rescuers." In addition, teachers—the true "gatekeepers of the young"—should be trained in the psychology of suicide prevention. . . .

In this ocean of sentiment and words, honest, thoughtful, popular reports on the real situation are almost nonexistent. However, numerous research articles appearing over the last ten years in professional social work and psychology journals have gone far toward explaining the youth suicide phenomenon, particularly the rise in the adolescent suicide rate between 1957 and 1977. Surprisingly, given the historic secular orientation of these professions, the journal articles testify to the critical role played by religious belief and family structure in preventing youth suicide.

No discussion of suicide research can begin, though, without attention to the work of French sociologist Emile Durkheim. . . .

Durkheim's Study

Durkheim focused on family and religion as the primary vehicles for collectivistic values. Concerning the former, he argued that a rise in the divorce rate would translate into a higher suicide rate. This would be particularly true among men, Durkheim reasoned, for while a man found his enjoyment "restricted" by marriage, "it is assured and this certainly forms his mental foundation." He also suggested that numerous children within a family would reduce the possibility of suicide. This would be particularly true for women, who tended to be more enmeshed in the daily flow of family life.

Turning to religion, Durkheim—himself a nonbeliever—argued that religion was not, in a sense, real. Rather, it was "the system of symbols by means of which society becomes conscious of itself; it is the characteristic way of thinking of collective existence." Dogma, in this view, was unimportant. Religion had meaning only as a mechanism for social cohesion.

In the modernizing world, Durkheim continued, even this role was decaying. As a means of imposing moral discipline on individuals, religion had already lost "most of its power" and would, in the future, decline further. The suicide rate would then rise. However, in a key turn of his argument, Durkheim stressed that the residual social function of religion could still be seen in the differential suicide rates of Catholics and Protestants. Catholics, he said, retained a relatively dense collective life, seen in a strict adherence to obligatory rituals and beliefs, which translated into higher integration and lower suicide rates. Protestants, in contrast, did not have to subordinate themselves to group ritual, and he theorized that their individualistic freedom would translate into a higher suicide rate. He compared suicide levels for Catholics and Protestants within five nations, and found that the rate of the latter was in all cases at least 50 percent higher. . . .

Negative Correlation

Sociologist Steven Stack of Auburn University [states] that Durkheim's reliance on religious affiliation (Catholic or Protestant) was inappropriate. Vastly more important to measuring re-

111

ligious effect on suicide was the degree of personal adherence to a core of "life-saving" beliefs. Religion, Stack noted, assuages all manner of human disappointments. Suffering is more readily endured if eternal salvation and heavenly glory are offered as reward to those who persevere. Belief that God is watching and cares about human suffering has a similar impact. Religious communities generate real concern among their members for those in trouble. The Bible offers solid role models, such as Job, for those who remain steadfast in suffering. Belief in Satan galvanizes individuals into common action against a shared enemy. Belief in a responsive God and the power of prayer also has measurable results. Stack concluded that if all else was equal and so long as religions encouraged these life-saving values, faith "will help to reduce suicide."

Finding a Correlation

The divorce rate tripled over the past twenty years, keeping pace with the adolescent suicide rate. More than half of American marriages now end in divorce—the highest rate in the world. A recent study found that only 38 percent of America's youth live with both natural parents. Although a causal relationship to suicide cannot be proved, of course, a correlation exists: While 50 percent of American couples eventually divorce, an estimated 70 percent of adolescents who attempt suicide come from divorced families.

George Howe Colt, *The Enigma of Suicide*, 1991.

On the far side of Durkheim, contemporary sociologists have rediscovered religion as the central explanatory factor in changes in suicide rates. Rodney Stark and his associates of the University of Washington, for example, have analyzed the relationship between church membership and suicide in the United States' 214 Standard Metropolitan Statistical Areas. They found "a very substantial and highly significant negative correlation" between the two, even after controlling for a series of variables (including rate of population growth, poverty level, and percent unemployed). In short, the higher the degree of church membership in a given urban area, the lower the suicide rate. In a remarkable study, Stack calculated the relationship between church attendance (persons being asked: "Did you, yourself, happen to attend church or synagogue in the last seven days?") and suicide rate. As expected, he found a significant and negative relationship between the two. He also discovered the most dramatic relationship between these two variables to be among young persons, ages 15 to 29. This group, he related, produced an almost perfect correlation: young Americans experienced both the sharpest drop in church attendance and the most rapid increase in suicide rate over this period. Notably, the church attendance decline was more closely associated with an increase in young female, rather than young male, suicides. Stack also calculated an "elasticity coefficient" which showed that a one percent increase in church attendance by young adults would translate into a 1.4 percent decrease in suicide. . . .

Such data point to a common conclusion: religious belief saves lives, particularly among women and youth.

Protection Against Suicide

Similar findings reaffirm the continued importance of traditional family life as a protection against suicide. A little-noticed paper published in 1976 confirmed what common sense suggests: the highest suicide rates are found among families with unmarried, divorced, or widowed parents; the lowest rate is found among intact nuclear families. Using nationwide data, psychologist David Lester found divorce rates to be the surest direct predictors of suicide rates. . . . Researchers found that marriage, while protecting both men and women from suicide, protected the former to a greater degree. A psychiatric team reported on the positive relationship between "a high incidence of early father loss," through divorce or illegitimacy, and suicidal behavior among young women. . . .

Here, too, research findings all point toward a common conclusion: the intact traditional family saves lives. . . .

Reclaiming Its Soul

Religion and the family are not mere options for this nation; they are necessities if the American republic is to survive and prosper. Hence, the solution to the youth suicide problem—indeed the solution to the largest share of our public problems—is the recovery of those two institutions which restrain and channel the individual life toward life, virtue, and community. . . .

Relative to social problems such as the self-destruction of youth, this does not mean that Americans can call on governments to restore vigorous religions and strong families. Such acts, of course, cannot be performed by the state. The important tasks must be addressed outside Washington. For those religious groups that succumbed in recent decades to the allure of political activism and to theologies shaped by ideological fads, the need is to recover fidelity to God's word and will. As modern social research suggests, stronger families would follow, the youth suicide rate would decline, and the Republic would reclaim its soul.

"There is no one explanation for the five thousand adolescent suicides each year."

There Is No Single Cause of Teen Suicide

George Howe Colt

In the following viewpoint, George Howe Colt states that there is no predominant cause of teen suicide. He points out that suicide is a symptom that occurs as a result of a number of biological, sociological, and psychological factors. Colt has written for the *New York Times* and *Harvard Magazine* and is currently a writer for *Life* magazine.

As you read, consider the following questions:

1. Why does Colt believe teen suicide is important even though the teen suicide rate is the lowest of any age group?
2. According to the author, what kinds of events contribute to teen suicide?
3. According to Colt, why don't most teenagers commit suicide?

Excerpted, with permission, from George Howe Colt's *The Enigma of Suicide*. New York: Summit Books, © 1991 by George Howe Colt.

For many years suicide was associated with older white males. Three times as many males as females commit suicide, and the rate rises with age. Statistics show that older white males are at the highest risk. Over the last three decades, however, a dramatic change has taken place. While the overall suicide rate has remained stable, the rate for adolescents (fifteen to twenty-four, as defined by federal statisticians) nearly tripled, from 4.5 suicides per 100,000 in 1950 to 13.6 per 100,000 in 1977. That year, 5,565 young men and women took their lives. (Under-reporting may be particularly prevalent for adolescents, for whom accidents are the leading cause of death, accounting for 40 percent of all fatalities.) During the last thirty years advances in medicine have lowered the mortality rate for every age group in America except fifteen-to-twenty-four-years-olds, whose rate has risen, largely because of the increase in suicides. "The real importance of this is that it shows a real, fundamental change in the phenomenon of suicide in this country," Mark Rosenberg, an epidemiologist at the Centers for Disease Control, told reporters. "Whereas a few years ago it might have been your grandfather . . . now it's your son."

More Demographics

While most of the attention has focused on teenagers, there are twice as many suicides in the college-age group (twenty to twenty-four) as among high school students (fifteen to nineteen), although the rate has risen remarkably for both. (There has been a 300 percent increase in the rate for ten-to-fourteen-year-olds.) Suicide is now the third leading cause of death among teenagers, behind accidents and homicides, and the second leading cause of death for twenty-to-twenty-four-year-olds, behind accidents. The increase can be narrowed down still further. Five times as many males as females kill themselves in this age group, compared to a three-to-one ratio in the population at large. One of every seven suicides in 1984 was a male between the ages of fifteen and twenty-four. Blacks of both sexes, young and old, commit suicide less frequently than whites, but the suicide rate of young black males has more than doubled in the last twenty-five years. Native Americans may have the highest adolescent suicide rate of any group. But the increase in the adolescent suicide rate is largely accounted for by white males twenty to twenty-four.

Suicide deaths represent the extreme range of adolescent suicidal behavior. Official statistics on attempted suicide are not kept, but studies estimate that for every adult suicide there are ten attempts; for every adolescent suicide there may be twenty or more. Psychologist Kim Smith of the Menninger Foundation, assembling data from several studies, suggests that 2 percent of all high schoolers have made at least one suicide attempt, which would mean that 2 million high schoolers, at some point in their lives, have attempted suicide. Most of them are female. While five times as many adolescent males as females kill themselves, three times as many females make attempts.

Youth Suicide Rate, 1950-1988

The youth suicide rate—expressed as the number of deaths per 100,000 population—has nearly tripled in the past 40 years. It rose from 4.5 in 1950 to 13.2 in 1988, the last year for which complete statistics are available. One fact has remained constant over the decades: White teenage boys and young men are far more likely to commit suicide than are other youths.

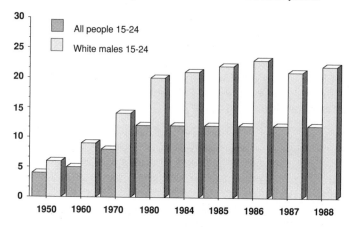

Source: Department of Health and Human Services, National Center for Health Statistics.

While some psychologists believe that nobody goes through adolescence without thinking of suicide at some point, it's clear that many young people have suicide on their minds. One study found 50 percent of teenagers have "seriously considered" suicide by the time they graduate high school; another study found 20 percent claimed they were "empty, confused, and would rather die than live." In a third study, 58 percent said they knew someone who had attempted suicide, and 10 percent had themselves made an attempt. And in a survey of high school and college students that asked, "Do you think suicide among young people is ever justified?" 49 percent said yes. Michael Peck, a Los Angeles psychiatrist who has studied adolescent suicide for more than two decades, asserts that up to 10 percent of the youngsters in any high school classroom may be considered at some risk for suicide; he believes more than 1 million adolescents enter suicidal crises each year.

Although many clinicians have been aware of the rising rate of adolescent suicide for more than two decades, only recently has national attention recognized the problem. That recognition was spurred by the growing suspicion that adolescent suicides tend to come in bunches. In 1983 when eight teenagers in fourteen months killed themselves in the wealthy Dallas suburb of Plano, teenage suicide became a big story. Suddenly, suicide seemed to be snatching, according to the media, "the best and the brightest" who had "everything to live for"—the football captain and the cheerleader as well as the loner or the delinquent. Across the country the questions poured out: Why was the adolescent suicide rate increasing so rapidly? Why these bunches of young suicides? Why are young people so unhappy? Why are they killing themselves?

A Symptom, Not a Disease

No one knows why people kill themselves. Trying to find the answer is like trying to pinpoint what causes us to fall in love or what causes war. There is no single answer. Suicide is not a disease like cancer or polio. It is a symptom. "The problem of suicide cuts across all diagnoses," says John Mack, a psychiatrist and coauthor of *Vivienne*, the story of a fourteen-year-old girl who hanged herself. "Some are mentally ill, most are not. Some are psychotic, most are not. Some are impulsive, most are not." Says psychologist Pamela Cantor, "People commit suicide for many reasons. Some people who are depressed will commit suicide, and some people who are schizophrenic will commit suicide, and some people who are fine but impulsive will commit suicide. We can't lump them all together." And just as there is no one explanation for the five thousand adolescent suicides each year, there is no one explanation for any particular suicide. While it is often said that suicide may be committed by twelve different people for twelve different reasons, it may be just as true to say that one person may choose death for twelve different reasons or one hundred different reasons—biological, sociological, and psychological factors that finally tighten around one place and time like a knot. . . .

Insufficient Explanations

Like the blind men who grab different parts of the elephant and misidentify the beast, suicide experts, exploring suicide from their own perspectives, end up supplying only part of the whole. "Suicide is a biological, sociocultural, interpersonal, dyadic, existential malaise," says Edwin Shneidman, a psychologist who has devoted his life to the study of suicide. Shneidman's definition is cumbersome, but it may be the most accurate we have. . . .

Most studies [of suicide] are retrospective—a researcher exam-

117

ines case histories of suicides hoping to find common characteristics. Finding commonalities, however, does not necessarily establish a causal relationship. Indeed, many clinicians say that,
given certain circumstances, we are all vulnerable to suicide. . . .

Numerous Reasons for Suicide

Little [can] explain the 300 percent rise in the adolescent suicide rate over the last three decades. To account for this "epidemic" of youth suicide, a host of explanations has been proposed: the unraveling of America's moral fiber, the breakdown
of the nuclear family, school pressure, peer pressure, parental
pressure, parental lassitude, child abuse, drugs, alcohol, low
blood sugar, TV, MTV, popular music (rock, punk, or Heavy
Metal, depending on the decade), promiscuity, lagging church
attendance, increased violence, racism, the Vietnam War, the
threat of nuclear war, the media, rootlessness, increased afflu-
ence, unemployment, capitalism, excessive freedom, boredom,
narcissism, Watergate, disillusionment with government, lack of
heroes, movies about suicide, too much discussion of suicide,
too little discussion of suicide. While none of these factors has
been proved to have more than an incidental correlation with
the rising rate of adolescent suicide, all of them represent very
real reasons why, as one psychiatrist says, "it may be more difficult to be a kid today than at any other time in history." . . .

Youth Suicides Increase

Approximately 18 teenagers kill themselves every day in this
country; and every hour about 57 adolescents unsuccessfully attempt self-engineered death. Much higher rates of teen suicide
are reported in Switzerland and Austria. Only car accidents cause
more deaths among adolescents than suicide, and many of these
may well be "autocides." Yet despite a number of recent federal,
state, and local programs attempting to address this problem, suicide remains a taboo subject for many parents. Sons and daugh-
ters may die by their own hands, but the deaths are rationalized
as Russian Roulette gone awry, accidental poisoning, or attributed to alcohol or drug abuse.

John Donnelly, ed., *Suicide: Right or Wrong,* 1990.

All of the factors mentioned as contributing to the increase in
suicide—divorce, rootlessness, increased competition—cause
stress and pain that may be expressed in a variety of self-destructive behaviors, all of which have increased over the last
three decades and all of which are correlated with increased

risk of suicide. They are connected to suicide like stars in a constellation. From 1960 to 1980, while the suicide rate for ages fifteen to twenty-four increased 136 percent, homicide deaths among the same age group increased by 164 percent. Arrests involving teenagers have doubled, and studies have found a high rate of previous suicide attempts among juvenile offenders. Studies of homeless and runaway youths have found an extraordinarily high instance of depression and attempted suicide. The pregnancy rate for Americans age fifteen to nineteen is 96 per thousand, more than double the rate of any other industrialized nation. More than 1 million adolescents become pregnant each year, and four out of five are unmarried. The suicide rate for teenage mothers is believed to be seven times greater than that for teenage girls without children. . . .

Why Most Teenagers Avoid Suicide

The vast majority of American teenagers, [however,] maneuver through adolescence without killing themselves. In 1984, for instance, 39,995,000 of 40,000,000 adolescents chose not to commit suicide. Although suicide is the second leading cause of death among adolescents, young people have the lowest suicide rate of any age group. While most people wonder why so many people commit suicide, some clinicians suggest that we have the question backward. Why don't more adolescents kill themselves? And why do so many consider it and then back away? Robert Litman, a psychiatrist at the Los Angeles Suicide Prevention Center, talks about something he calls "the suicide zone." He believes that suicide-vulnerable individuals move in and out of periods of suicidal risk—sometimes for brief periods, sometimes for moderate or long periods—as their life circumstances fluctuate. But of all those people who enter that zone, very few actually kill themselves. "For every hundred people at high risk," he says, "only three or four will actually commit suicide over the next couple of years."

For that to happen, says Litman, a multitude of things must occur. "It's like a slot machine," he says. "You can win a million dollars on a slot machine in Las Vegas, but to do that, six sevens have to line up on your machine. That happens only once in a million times. In a sense it's the same with suicide." Those spinning sevens represent all the biological, sociological, psychological, and existential variables that are associated with suicide—broken family, locus of control, decreased serotonin, triggering event, and so on. "In order to commit suicide, a lot of things have to fall together at once, and a lot of other things have to *not* happen at once," says Litman. "There's a certain random element determining the specific time of any suicide and, often, whether it happens or not."

In Litman's slot machine metaphor, suicide is seen as an exceedingly rare event that requires everything to be in alignment for it to take place—a sort of perverse, malevolent music of the spheres. "It's as if you need to have six strikes against you," Litman says. "And we're all walking around with one or two or three strikes. Then you get into a big crisis and you have four strikes. But to get to all six really takes some bad luck."

a critical thinking activity

Distinguishing Between Fact and Opinion

This activity is designed to help develop the basic reading and thinking skill of distinguishing between fact and opinion. Consider the following statement as an example: "More than one thousand adolescents aged 18 to 19 years intentionally killed themselves with firearms in 1988." This is a factual statement because it could be checked by looking at the method of youth suicide in government health statistics. But the statement "The solution to the youth suicide problem is the recovery of religion and the family" is an opinion. Many people may not think religion and family can solve teen suicide. Others might even argue that religion and family can sometimes present problems that cause teens to commit suicide.

When investigating controversial issues, it is important that one be able to distinguish between statements of fact and statements of opinion. It is also important to recognize that not all statements of fact are true. They may appear to be true, but some are based on inaccurate or false information. For this activity, however, we are concerned with understanding the difference between those statements that appear to be factual and those that appear to be based primarily on opinion.

Most of the following statements are taken from the viewpoints in this chapter. Consider each statement carefully. *Mark O for any statement you believe is an opinion or interpretation of facts. Mark F for any statement you believe is a fact. Mark I for any statement you believe is impossible to judge.*

If you are doing this activity as a member of a class or group, compare your answers with those of other class or group members. Be able to defend your answers. You may discover that others come to different conclusions than you do. Listening to the reasons others present for their answers may give you valuable insights into distinguishing between fact and opinion.

O = *opinion*
F = *fact*
I = *impossible to judge*

1. In the study, eight of the suicide victims had rifles available to them, and six used these weapons to kill themselves.

2. Religion and family are necessities if America is to survive and prosper.

3. Divorce rates are the surest direct predictors of suicide rates.

4. Religion presents a risk in gay youth suicide because of its depiction of homosexuality as a sin.

5. In 1977, 5,565 young men and women committed suicide.

6. The response of our society as a whole to homosexuality poses the greatest risk to gay and lesbian youth.

7. Suicide is now the third leading cause of death among teenagers.

8. Five times as many males as females kill themselves in the fifteen to twenty-four-year age group.

9. The stress resulting from major life changes undoubtedly taxes the adolescent's coping skills and contributes to the rate of suicide.

10. More restrictive gun control laws would reduce the suicide rate among adolescents.

11. Restrictive gun control laws would not reduce the suicide rate.

12. The 300 percent increase in teen suicide indicates an epidemic of youths taking their lives.

13. It is impossible to study suicide from the point of view of those who commit it, since they are dead.

14. Physicians have a responsibility to make a clear and firm recommendation that firearms be removed from the homes of suicide-risk youths.

15. Suicide completion is a much rarer phenomenon than suicide attempt.

16. It is more difficult to be a teenager today than at any other time in history.

17. About 30 percent of the million attempted teen suicides each year are committed by gays and lesbians.

18. Three times as many females as males attempt suicide.

Periodical Bibliography

The following articles have been selected to supplement the diverse views presented in this chapter.

Mary Billard	"Heavy Metal Goes on Trial," *Rolling Stone*, July 12-26, 1990.
Samuel L. Blumenfeld	"The Teenage Suicide Holocaust: Is Death Education the Cause?" *The Blumenfeld Education Letter*, July 1990. Available from PO Box 45161, Boise, ID 83711.
Frank E. Crumley	"Substance Abuse and Adolescent Suicidal Behavior," *Journal of the American Medical Association*, June 13, 1990. Available from American Medical Association, Division of Publishing Operations, 515 N. State St., Chicago, IL 60610.
Suzette Greenhagen	"That's No Way to End a Good Life," *Newsweek*, special edition, Summer/Fall 1990.
William A. Henry and Erik Pappa	"Did the Music Say 'Do It'?" *Time*, July 30, 1990.
Journal of the American Medical Association	"Youth Suicide: The Physician's Role in Suicide Prevention," December 26, 1990.
Fran McGovern	"Children in the Abyss," *The American Legion*, April 1991. Available from Membership Processing Dept., PO Box 1954, Indianapolis, IN 46206.
Newsweek	"Blaming Death on Hidden Messages," July 30, 1990.
Anna Quindlen	"Suicide Solution," *The New York Times*, September 30, 1990.
Joan E. Rigdon	"Asian-American Youth Suffer a Rising Toll from Heavy Pressures," *The Wall Street Journal*, July 10, 1991.
Mark L. Rosenberg, James A. Mercy, and Vernon N. Houk	"Guns and Adolescent Suicides," *Journal of the American Medical Association*, December 4, 1991.
Phyllis Schlafly	"Suicide Courses Are Dangerous to Children," *Conservative Chronicle*, December 23, 1991. Available from PO Box 11297, Des Moines, IA 50340-1297.
Susan E. Swedo	"Tracking Teen Suicide Attempters," *Science News*, October 5, 1991.
Nancy Wartik	"Jerry's Choice: Why Are Our Children Killing Themselves?" *American Health*, October 1991.

How Can Suicide Be Prevented?

Chapter Preface

Suicide prevention today focuses on educating the public and offering compassion to the suicidal. This method is a fairly recent phenomenon. Not until the twentieth century and the creation of the National Save-a-Life League in the United States did society consider reaching out to, rather than condemning, potential suicide victims. The league, established in 1906 by Baptist minister Harry Marsh Warren, offered compassionate counseling, money, and shelter to the suicidal. Through his work, Warren found that about two-thirds of the suicidal did not need psychiatric help but simply needed someone who would listen to their grievances. The league estimates that between 1906 and 1940 it saved at least thirty-four thousand lives.

Similar agencies were quickly established throughout the United States and Europe. The Salvation Army founded the London Anti-Suicide Bureau in England, while in Vienna the Ethical Society Agency for Suicidal Persons provided counseling and social services to despondent adults and adolescents. These agencies were not only effective at preventing suicide, but also at mediating family disputes, assisting the destitute, and helping the lonely develop social ties.

The world's largest suicide prevention organization, the Samaritans, was established in England in 1953. While many other prevention organizations focused on providing counseling to the suicidal, the Samaritans created a unique one-on-one approach in which each volunteer befriended a client to form a lasting friendship. The Samaritans found this system to be very effective and consequently began to expand the organization. Today there are Samaritan branches in at least forty-four nations.

Most suicide prevention groups such as the Samaritans adhere to the belief, expressed by Voltaire, that "the man, who in a fit of melancholy, kills himself today, would have wished to live had he waited a week." Armed with the knowledge that the desire to commit suicide is often temporary, those involved in suicide prevention work to help despondent people find solutions to their problems or relief from their pain before they consider or resort to suicide.

While prevention workers clearly offer a valuable service to those who are depressed, in recent years they have come under attack for being unprofessional and ineffective at preventing suicide. Statistics show that even with the tremendous growth in suicide prevention centers in the past thirty years there has been no corresponding dramatic decrease in the suicide rate. Critics speculate that this is because suicide prevention volunteers are ill-equipped to deal with the suicidal. Other studies show, however, that prevention centers attract callers who are less likely to kill themselves, but who need to talk to someone because of a temporary crisis. Consequently, while prevention workers may be unable to help people who are chronically depressed, suicidal, and in need of intensive therapy, they do provide a service to many people facing temporary traumas.

The authors in the following chapter discuss the effectiveness of suicide prevention centers and other ways to prevent suicide.

"Suicide prevention centers do, in fact, help prevent suicide."

Suicide Prevention Centers Can Help Prevent Suicide

George Howe Colt

The effectiveness of suicide prevention centers is a controversial issue. While those who establish such centers may have good intentions, many researchers believe the centers do nothing to decrease the suicide rate. In the following viewpoint, George Howe Colt disagrees. Colt, who describes the efforts of suicide prevention centers, believes such centers do prevent some desperate people from killing themselves. Colt, a writer for *Life* magazine, has written for the *New York Times* and for *Harvard Magazine*.

As you read, consider the following questions:

1. What kind of people call suicide prevention centers, according to the author?
2. How are suicide prevention centers expanding their services, according to Colt?
3. Other than suicide prevention, what does the author believe is the most important service offered by suicide prevention centers?

Excerpted, with permission, from George Howe Colt's *The Enigma of Suicide*. New York: Summit Books, © 1991 by George Howe Colt.

127

The phone rings in a small room in a one-story building in Los Angeles. Pat, a trim, forty-three-year-old woman wearing sneakers, jeans, and a sweatshirt, picks up the receiver and in a warm, gentle voice says, "Hello, may I help you?" As she listens to the answer, she becomes still. "Nine Percodans? I don't know," she says. "I'm not a doctor. . . . Did you take nine Percodans? Did someone you know take them?" After each question Pat listens intently before asking the next. "How old is your friend? . . . Nineteen? . . . Is she there with you? . . . No? . . . How frightening." Pat speaks slowly, her voice comforting but firm. "Your friend should get some help. Do you have anyone to call who can help you with this? . . . Maybe you should call the paramedics. Did you call her house? . . . She has roommates? . . . Might they know where she is? . . . Might she call you back? . . . No? . . . She just called you to say good-bye?"

Pat puts on her glasses as if it might help her focus even more closely on the caller. If she feels any tension, her voice doesn't betray it. "Do you have any idea where she might be, places she might go? . . . Does she have a car? . . . Does she have any family? . . . Have you called them? . . . They're looking for her? . . . What's your friend's name?" Pat's voice softens. "Is it that you don't want to give her last name? . . . If she calls us, can we call you?" Pat pauses a moment. "Are you frightened? . . . What of? . . . We're not the police. And even if we were, it's not against the law to kill yourself. . . . Is there anything I can do to help *you*?" Pat's head bows over the desk. "If you *are* Susan or if you have taken the Percodan, you need to get to the hospital immediately." There is a brief silence and then the sound of weeping spills from the phone. "What has happened?" says Pat with infinite tenderness. "Why do you want to die?"

Assessing the Situation

It is 10 p.m. on a Tuesday night in April. Pat is sitting on the edge of a plastic swivel chair, leaning over a desk in a corner of the "telephone room" at the Institute for Studies of Destructive Behaviors and the Suicide Prevention Center, commonly known as the Los Angeles Suicide Prevention Center. The LASPC is one of the oldest and most famous of this country's suicide prevention centers. Pat is a volunteer on its twenty-four-hour crisis line. . . .

As Pat tries to comfort the girl, she gathers information, trying to assess how lethal the situation is and what supports the girl might have to help her through this crisis. Like a climber struggling for a foothold on a steep rock face, she searches for a way to establish a connection with this girl. Though the girl sounds timid, despair makes her stubborn: She keeps coming back to her first question—will the nine Percodans kill her or leave her a cripple?

"Any medication could kill you; I don't have that information," Pat says. "Where is your pain coming from? Is it physical? . . . Have you spoken to anyone about it? . . . Does your therapist know how you're feeling? . . . You called her? She's away? . . ." Pat shakes her head. "I don't know. I don't have that kind of training—and even a doctor won't give you that information over the phone. . . . Do you live with your family? . . . Are you close to your father? . . . How about your mother? . . . Have you talked to her about this? . . . Why not? . . . What would she say if you told her? . . ." Pat twists slightly in her chair. "It must be hard when those you love are so far away from how you're feeling." She is silent for a moment, listening to the girl's quick anxious breaths. "You don't trust me at all, do you?" says Pat kindly. "I won't hurt you—I promise that."

The Suicide Prevention Worker

An active suicide prevention service has a limited goal. It provides a ready contact between the community's highly disturbed citizens and the established helping agencies that are available to them.

When a person calls to say that he or she is contemplating suicide, the voice of the suicide prevention worker on the other end can become the caller's lifeline.

Edwin S. Shneidman and Philip Mandelkorn, *How to Prevent Suicide*, 1967.

This is the eleventh call Pat has taken since beginning her six-hour shift at 6:30. The Crisis Line at the LASPC receives an average of sixty to seventy calls a day from people who are lonely, depressed, angry, and perhaps suicidal. The lines are open twenty-four hours a day, 365 days a year. The LASPC is the only suicide prevention center or twenty-four-hour general-purpose crisis line in Los Angeles County. When other hot lines and therapists close up shop for the day, many of them leave the LASPC number on their answering machines for callers in crisis after office hours. Although the LASPC has four incoming lines, the phone company has told the center that during its busiest hours, 7 p.m. to 1 a.m.—the time when most suicides occur—callers must sometimes dial five or six times before they can get through.

A Range of Problems

The LASPC keeps careful records of who calls and why. They have learned that calls come from as wide a range of people and problems as seem to exist. More than 60 percent are from the troubled person himself. The rest are from third-party callers—concerned relatives and friends, or therapists seeking advice on how to handle a suicidal client. Two-thirds of the calls are from women. While the majority of calls come from the Los Angeles area, calls have come from as far away as Iowa, Florida, and France. Ten percent of their calls are from people under the age of twenty. Once, an eight-year-old boy called. He was lonely, he told the counselor. His mother traveled a lot on business, and he worried that he was the reason she was never home. Later, the counselor called the boy's mother. She was initially outraged at the intrusion, but when she realized that her son had been upset enough to call a suicide prevention center, she listened.

Although the notion of a suicide prevention center may conjure images of heroic volunteers talking desperate people into putting down a loaded gun, the majority of calls are much less dramatic. Most callers to the LASPC or to any of the over two hundred suicide prevention centers in the United Sates are not in immediate danger of killing themselves. This has led some critics to suggest that most people who call a prevention center don't really want to die. The LASPC agrees. They believe that even the most desperately suicidal people are ambivalent—a part of them wants to live, and a part of them wants to die. By calling the center they have issued a "cry for help." Nevertheless, many of those who call the center are at risk for suicide. A previous attempt is the most accurate predictor for subsequent suicide, and half of the people who call the LASPC have made previous attempts. Twelve percent of callers are considered to be at high risk; that is, they are so distressed that the LASPC believes they would have made an attempt within forty-eight hours if they had not called. Three percent of callers have already swallowed pills or cut their wrists when they call the center and may die unless the LASPC gets them immediate help. . . .

Problems with a Relationship

The girl is no longer crying, but her breathing is heavy. Slowly, Pat has established a thin ledge of trust. "Did something happen tonight?" she asks. "Can you tell me what that was? . . . Was it something someone said? . . . Who?" After each question Pat lets the girl's answer settle for a moment before continuing. "What did he say? . . . Have you talked to him about it? What kind of compromises? . . . Sexual things? . . . Is this the person you want to spend your life with? . . . You care too much for him to leave him, but you have a hard time staying with him?" Pat pauses. "You know, suicide is a permanent solution to a temporary problem. . . . Is your fiancé in counseling? . . . Do you think you're ready to share your life with someone who thinks he's perfect? . . . Would it be so terrible to end your relationship with him rather than end your life? . . . Why? . . . How do you know you can't live without him? . . . You tried? . . . Maybe a month isn't enough. . . . Everything changes. Nothing stays the same." Pat hunches over, her elbows on her knees. "Have you ever told him you were thinking of killing yourself? . . . What does he say? . . . He doesn't believe you? . . . Have you talked to him tonight? . . . How did you end the conversation?" Pat listens to the answer, then repeats it softly to herself, nodding. "Sweet dreams.". . .

Improved Mental Health

There is no doubt that carefully established suicide prevention services pay off in lives and money saved. Community mental health improves as a result. Each community should tailor a sui-cide prevention service to its own needs.

Edwin S. Shneidman and Philip Mandelkorn, *How to Prevent Suicide*, 1967.

Most suicide prevention lines base their work on "active listening," a technique generally attributed to the psychologist Carl Rogers, founder of "client-centered therapy." In "active listening" the listener affirms what the caller is feeling. If the caller says, "I feel really awful," the listener might say, "it sounds as though you're feeling pretty awful." As the caller vents his feelings, the volunteer listens actively until the crisis has passed, then perhaps offers a referral. In fact, the LASPC's active listening has become a little more active in recent years. The staff has found that an increasing number of their callers are chronic, and counselors are urged to make sure that repeat callers have followed through on previous recommendations. At other centers volunteers are "workers," "listeners," or "befrienders"; at the LASPC they are "counselors." The LASPC counselor is trained not merely to listen but to probe, to ask questions, to solicit information, and to sort through options with the caller. . . .

Occasionally, a caller is in a crisis in which he cannot be helped to help himself, and more direct intervention is needed. While a few prevention centers do not trace calls or intervene with third-party callers to preserve confidentiality, the LASPC traces calls and often intervenes in third-party situations. About once a week an LASPC counselor must send the police or an ambulance to a caller's home. In keeping with their philosophy of helping the clients to help themselves, the counselor will first try to get the caller or someone else in the home to take such action or at least agree to let the counselor do so. If the caller refuses to give his address, the counselor will try to keep him on the line long enough to trace the call (which can take several hours) and dispatch emergency help.

Beyond the Call of Duty

More often, however, a counselor will maneuver behind the scenes. Recently, crisis line coordinator Beverly Kalasardo was on the line when a fifteen-year-old girl called in tears. Her boyfriend had just received his grades and realized he was going to fail. Making her promise not to tell anyone, he told the girl he had a shotgun and was going to kill himself. Kalasardo calmed the girl as they tried to find a solution. They couldn't talk to the boy's parents; his father was an abusive alcoholic, and his mother wouldn't have cared. They couldn't talk to her parents; they didn't like the boy either. Kalasardo asked the girl if she would feel comfortable talking to the school counselor. The girl said no. "I asked her if I could, and she said yes," recalls Kalasardo. "So I called the counselor and explained the problem. Meanwhile, the girl talked to their friends, who walked the boy from class to class. The counselor called the boy in, and without letting him know he knew about his plans for suicide, told him he had been looking at his grades, and while it was a shame they were low, he could go to summer school and pull them up without hurting his record. The boy hadn't thought of this option and was relieved. He told the girl. She called me. Later, she wrote me a nice thank-you letter.". . .

It is past eleven. As the city of Los Angeles begins to fall asleep, the volunteers at the LASPC are trying to put people to bed, like air traffic controllers trying to talk pilots down through heavy storms for a safe landing. But some do not want to come down and end up circling, circling. As the call continues, Pat leans still lower over the desk and holds the phone even tighter against her ear, as if by sheer will she might be able to squeeze into the telephone cord and travel through the wires across Los Angeles to some unknown room and sit beside this nineteen-year-old girl. They have been talking for more than an hour. Pat can feel the girl, like a fish on a line, pull away, then come closer, then pull away again. Pat is trying different approaches, her voice now a little softer, now probing, nudging, but never losing its concern. She asks fewer questions now and offers more suggestions. Although the girl has opened up a little, her voice is still a small, thin monotone, and she keeps coming back to the Percodan and whether nine will be enough.

"Are you determined to take those nine Percodan?" Pat asks. "I can't stop you. I hope you don't do that. . . . I think you're making a mistake. . . . It's going to take a little more strength to choose a different option." Her voice becomes firmer. "No, you haven't. You have *not* tried everything. . . . I suspect you're stronger than you sound. . . . I think you deny your strength." Pat senses the girl retreating. "I can't give you anything you don't already have," says Pat. "But I don't want you to hurt yourself. I don't want you to kill yourself. . . . Do you think you can get through tonight?" She pauses. . . . "If you're thinking of killing yourself at any point again, will you call us first? . . . Will you? . . ." As the girl apologizes for taking up so much of her time and thanks her for listening, Pat imperceptibly shakes her head, then says softly, "Thank you for calling."

A Feeling of Defeat

After the girl hangs up, Pat holds the phone in midair, staring at it as if more words or tears might still pour out. Then she gently sets it in its cradle. She lets out a deep sigh. "Oh, mercy," she says. It is 11:20, and she has been on the phone for eighty minutes. "I think she's going to kill herself," she says, "or at least make an attempt," and for the first time since she took the call Pat sounds tense, tired, and a bit defeated. "I told her I can't keep her from killing herself, but also you have to remember you can't make her kill herself." She shrugs. "You have to hold on to that, working here." Pat shakes her head slowly, sadly. "She hung up crying, and when I picked up the call, she was crying.". . .

Studies show that most calls to prevention centers are not from the severely suicidal. In a 1970 study of ten centers, 33 percent of their callers had been considering suicide, and the percentage of seriously suicidal callers was far smaller. More than half of the four thousand calls received monthly at the Suicide Prevention and Crisis Center in Buffalo, for example, were from crank callers, pranksters, or people who hung up immediately. The majority of suicides are older white males; the majority of prevention center callers are young white females. Although some suggest that most people are simply not aware that prevention centers exist, a study by San Francisco psychiatrist Jerome Motto found that while 80 percent of a group of depressed and suicidal persons had heard of the local prevention center, only 11 percent had used it. Suicidal people, reasons sociologist Ronald Maris, are simply too isolated to call a stranger.

Yet prevention centers clearly get many high-risk callers. At the LASPC, several follow-up studies have shown that about 1 percent of callers kill themselves within two years. Although these figures may be interpreted several ways, they indicate that prevention centers work with a high-risk group: Callers represent about one hundred times as great a risk of suicide as the general population. . . .

Meanwhile, prevention centers continue to refine their ser-

133

vices. In an attempt to reach a greater number of high-risk callers, prevention centers have developed programs for specific target groups. Some centers operate special lines for AIDS, child abuse, rape, the homeless, gays, and lesbians. Some offer group therapy for the suicidal or support groups for bereaved family and friends left behind after a suicide. Others run training and education programs for the police, the military, or high school and college students. San Francisco Suicide Prevention runs a special twenty-four-hour hot line for the elderly, including regular callbacks and home visits. The Samaritans of Boston helped organize a suicide prevention program at the Charles Street Jail in which inmates befriend other inmates.

Saving Lives

Although prevention centers no longer make exaggerated claims of efficacy, recent evidence confirms that suicide prevention centers do, in fact, help prevent suicide. A 1984 University of Alabama study comparing suicide rates in Alabama counties that had a center with those that did not, found that the centers were associated with a reduction of suicides by young white females—the demographic group to which most callers belong. Extrapolating their calculations to include the entire nation, they estimate that suicide prevention centers save the lives of 637 young white females each year.

With or without statistical reinforcement, the value of prevention centers should not be assessed solely by the suicide rate. While the word suicide is prominent in their advertising and an estimated one-third of their callers are suicidal, suicidality is not a prerequisite for calling the LASPC or any other suicide prevention center. But if what keeps people alive is connection, centers may provide a small dose of caring that may prevent someone's loneliness from spiraling into suicide months or years down the line. "Most callers are lonely, frightened, desperate people who don't know where to turn, and when they call the center, at least they get some sort of answering voice," says Robert Litman. "That's not necessarily suicide prevention, but it does play a part in stabilizing society. It is a little bit of society's answer to the chaos that society creates." Just as Nietzsche said the thought of suicide "helps one through many a dreadful night," the thought of a suicide prevention center has gotten many thousands of people through their own dreadful nights. David Klugman remembers one of the first calls he handled at the LASPC. When he picked up the phone and said, "Hello, may I help you?", there was a silence. Then a timid voice on the other end said, "I can't talk now. . . . I just needed to know someone's there."

"School districts have been charged with the responsibility of developing curricula . . . that will specifically address suicide prevention. "

Education Can Help Prevent Suicide

Judith M. Stillion, Eugene E. McDowell, and Jacque H. May

In the following viewpoint, Judith M. Stillion, Eugene E. Mc-Dowell, and Jacque H. May assert that schools can help prevent suicide by teaching students coping skills that will help them solve problems in ways other than by killing themselves. Both Stillion and McDowell have written extensively on the topic of suicide. Stillion is a professor at Western Carolina University in Cullowhee, North Carolina. McDowell is director of the Asheville Graduate Center of the University of North Carolina. May has her master's degree in clinical psychology.

As you read, consider the following questions:

1. Why are many American children incapable of dealing with life's stresses, in the authors' opinion?
2. What problems occur when individual school systems require suicide prevention courses but are unable to solicit expert help, according to the authors?
3. What role do the authors believe parents can play in suicide prevention?

Excerpted from *Suicide Across the Life Span: Premature Exits* by Judith M. Stillion, Eugene E. McDowell, and Jacque H. May. Philadelphia: Hemisphere Books, 1989. Reprinted with permission from Hemisphere Books, a member of the Taylor & Francis Group.

It is clear from the suicide statistics in the United States that our society is failing to teach young people (especially young white males) how to cope in a healthy fashion with the stresses inherent in living in a complex technological society. While an in-depth discussion of coping techniques is beyond the scope of this viewpoint, it is important to summarize the minimum content of a general curriculum designed to prepare young people to live out their full life spans.

First, students should be made aware of the complexities involved in living and of the inevitability of experiencing some failure, disappointment, and loss in life. Because caring adults want to protect children whenever possible from harsh realities, some children may come to adolescence with little expectation of encountering adversities in life and may therefore be unprepared to face such adversities. On the other hand, some children born into turbulent homes or growing up in conditions of poverty may face severe problems before having an opportunity to learn how to cope. Thus, there is a need to teach healthy coping techniques to children from both extremes. The school may be their last best chance to observe competent models and learn these important skills.

The way in which teachers handle failure experiences is particularly crucial. Students should be specifically taught not to internalize failure in such a way that they denigrate themselves and weaken their own self-esteem. Educators interested in developing positive coping techniques will help students to view failure as a form of feedback that can lead to future success and to view disappointment as a temporary state that can, with effort and understanding, lead to greater accomplishment.

Learning to Cope

Second, specific coping techniques should be explored with young people. Such exploration might include an examination of coping strategies presently used by students when they feel depressed. An exercise conducted recently with a group of academically gifted ninth graders yielded no less than 23 coping mechanisms they employed to help themselves feel better. Coping mechanisms mentioned frequently included exercising, eating, talking with friends, listening to music, writing out their feelings in diaries or in letters to friends, composing poetry, taking long walks, focusing on the pluses in their lives, and talking with parents, counselors, and other adults. It is important to help students see that they already have a repertoire of coping techniques and therefore a base for developing stronger and more varied approaches to coping with stress.

Among the additional coping techniques that can be taught is the skill of critical thinking. Support for teaching critical thinking has been spreading during the 1980s. The rationale for teaching this skill is generally economic (i.e., our society needs people who are good problem solvers and who can critically analyze situations and products and can contribute new ideas). We believe that training in critical thinking is also training in flexible thinking. Cognitive constriction often accompanies suicidal thought patterns. Students who form a habit early of analyzing situations from a variety of perspectives, of asking appropriate questions, and of testing the realism of their own thinking are far less likely to settle easily into the cognitive inflexibility that focuses on suicide as *the* solution.

The Ability to Laugh

Encouraging students to develop a sense of humor is another technique for preventing suicide. People who can laugh at themselves and at many of life's problems are in a good position to avoid the deadly serious type of thinking involved in suicide. It is difficult to remain depressed if you can see humor in a situation. Young children generally appreciate humor. Interested adults and school curricula that build upon this natural appreciation for the humorous are inoculating children against suicide.

Table 1: School Suicide Prevention Activities in the United States

Prevention activities and materials	Provided by statewide education offices	Developed by individual school systems
1. Materials for teaching about suicide	17 (37%)	32 (70%)
2. Curriculum guidelines for suicide prevention	9 (20%)	35 (76%)
3. Policies and procedures for dealing with student response to a suicide crisis	5 (11%)	38 (83%)

Helping children and adolescents to set high but attainable goals for themselves is another technique that promotes coping. In recent years, this technique has been shown to be associated with achievement in the classroom. We think it is also a powerful deterrent to suicide. Young people, who experience a wide gulf between who they are and who they want to become, are at risk for low self-concepts, self-hatred, depression, and suicidal behavior. Helping adults can encourage growing children to set short-range, realistic goals and can support them as they work toward reaching these goals. Achievement enhances self-esteem and helps students appreciate their own worth and uniqueness.

As students come to view themselves as increasingly competent, they will be less likely to develop on the negative end of Erik Erikson's latency stage, with its extremes of industry versus inferiority. In this way, achievement and competence become two powerful tools of suicide prevention.

Other skills that can be taught to children to help them cope with stress include specific techniques such as systematic relaxation, imagery techniques, meditation, and positive self-talk. All such techniques help students attain control over stress, and they also arm them with behavioral choices other than giving in to depressed or suicidal feelings.

Education for Suicide Prevention

The second major education need is for suicide prevention education. The public schools in the United States have always been expected to provide many services in addition to the education of our youth. In the past 30 years, however, the number of these special, nonacademic responsibilities has increased. The public schools have been asked to address concerns ranging from the mundane (e.g., a "swish and spit" program of oral hygiene) to the momentous (e.g., the racial integration of our society). During the 1980s, many school districts have been charged with the responsibility of developing curricula and procedures that will specifically address suicide prevention among children and adolescents in the United States.

At the beginning of the decade, few school-based suicide prevention programs existed. A few pioneer programs, such as those of the Cherry Creek school system in Denver and the Fairfax County public schools in Virginia, were in the process of being developed. These programs have now become well established and are viewed as national models. By the mid-1980s, the increasing awareness of the growing adolescent suicide problem and the special risk of cluster suicides among this age group led to the rapid development of many school-based programs. Community health professionals, parent groups, legislators, and educators themselves lent their voices to the growing advocacy for suicide prevention programs in the public schools. Their requests gained in salience when parents of suicide victims in several states (e.g., California and Oregon) sued school districts over the lack of suicide prevention training for teachers. Although the legal issues regarding school liability are far from settled, a landmark decision in a federal court in 1985 held that parents of a youth suicide may sue a school if the death allegedly resulted from inadequate staff training in suicide prevention (*Kelson v. City of Springfield, Oregon 767* F.2d 651 [Ninth Circuit Court of Appeals]). Also, legislation mandating the establishment of suicide prevention programs in the schools has been passed in at least six states: California, Florida, Louisiana, Maryland, New Jersey, and Wisconsin. Many other states, including Kentucky, Rhode Island, Missouri, Minnesota, Pennsylvania, and Oregon, have commissioned special task forces to study the youth suicide problem and to develop guidelines for suicide prevention to be used in developing programs for individual school systems.

Surveying Schools

In an attempt to discover how organized the increased interest in education for suicide prevention had become at the state level, we planned and carried out a survey of the 50 state superintendents of public instruction in the United States during the fall of 1987. The brief survey sent to these offices included questions concerning the development of materials and the availability of curriculum guidelines for teaching about suicide and questions about the development of policies and procedures for dealing with the response to a student suicide or suicide attempt among peers. Although the survey was primarily designed to gather information concerning activities at the state level, respondents were also asked to provide information concerning delegation of these responsibilities to individual school systems. The findings from the surveys, which were returned by 46 of the 50 state departments of public instruction, are summarized in Table 1.

Table 1 shows that although much ongoing suicide prevention activity exists in the public schools, responsibility for these activities falls heavily on individual school systems, with only limited direction from the state departments of public instruction. Only 37% of the state education offices provide individual school systems with materials for teaching about suicide, and only 20% provide curriculum guidelines for suicide prevention. The table also shows that even fewer statewide systems (11%) are involved in the development of policies and procedures for dealing with the student response to a suicide or a suicide attempt.

All state departments of public instruction were asked to include with the completed questionnaire a copy of any suicide prevention guidelines developed by their offices. We received such materials from only 15 states. Of the sets of guidelines received, 11 dealt specifically with suicide prevention and 4 contained general health curriculum guidelines. . . .

Although the specific contents of these guidelines differed

139

from state to state, most programs included guidelines for classroom instruction and for teacher and staff training workshops. The in-service training guidelines addressed issues associated with prevention, intervention, and postvention.

Assessing the Risk of Suicide

The materials from the state education offices included guidelines for pupil services also. The recommended guidelines included procedures for identification of suicidal students and risk assessment. Recommendations for risk assessment included using procedures such as the SAL method of inquiry with suspected suicidal youth (specificity of plan, availability of means, and lethality of method). The guidelines also included referral procedures (e.g., keep the student with a responsible adult, inform the parents). Finally, many guidelines included crisis response procedures to reduce the likelihood of cluster or copycat suicides (e.g., establish a crisis management team before a tragedy occurs, meet with high-risk students in small groups or individually, designate one person to talk to the press).

Saving a Valuable Resource

The young people in our schools are society's most valuable—and valued—resource. When a young person dies by his or her own hand, more than the life, and future life, of that person is lost. So, too, is a measure of hope.

Educators, administrators, and counselors working in schools all have a responsibility to take action, not only on behalf of the individuals who are at risk, but also in aid and support of those around them. For every individual who needs direct and immediate help, there are many more who need assistance in knowing what they can do that will make a difference.

Although there still are unanswered questions (and pitfalls to avoid), there is still a knowledge base to guide action. Working in our communities, with care, carefulness, and compassion, school personnel can move forward to learn more about preventing the tragic and early death of young people and to incorporate in their schools the policies, programs, and practices that offer the best hope of preventing this loss.

Cheryl J. Vince and Kimberly R. Hamrick, eds., *Youth Suicide: Issues, Assessment, and Intervention*, 1990.

In addition to curriculum, in-service training, and pupil services guidelines, the materials provided by the state departments of public instruction usually included descriptions of model programs, bibliographical material, a list of community resources, referral and reporting forms, and a list of suicide prevention resources. . . .

The suicide prevention program guidelines received from the state education offices were well prepared, complete, and very helpful for individual school systems preparing their own programs. In spite of the quality of the materials received, however, the fact that so few state departments of public instruction provide direction for individual school systems is a matter of continuing concern. Too often individual school systems are mandated to develop comprehensive programs to deal with the youth suicide problem without adequate directions and guidelines from the state. While respect for the autonomy of individual school systems is praiseworthy, absence of direction from and lack of accountability to the state education offices result in unevenness of quality and fragmentation of efforts.

Comparisons to Canada

Moving from the state level to the level of individual schools, a special task force of the American Association on Suicidology recently conducted a survey of 158 school-related suicide programs in the United States and Canada (Smith, Eyman, Dyck, & Ryerson, 1987). The survey showed few differences between U.S. and Canadian school-based suicide programs. In fact, the only consistent difference found between programs in the two countries was one of emphasis. The Canadian programs tend to focus on education while U.S. programs emphasize both education and crisis intervention.

Sixty percent of the 158 school-related suicide prevention programs surveyed included units about youth suicide designed for teachers to use in classroom instruction. Although some programs included curricula for all 12 grades, the majority focused on junior high school and high school students. Most curricula emphasized giving students practical information, such as facts, signs, symptoms, and referral sources. Most of the curricula also included help in developing coping skills, such as the identification and acceptance of one's own feelings, and techniques for responding to a friend's suicidal crisis. Approximately one-third of the school-related suicide programs surveyed included an instructional component containing materials to be used with school nurses, counselors, school social workers, and parents. One quarter of the programs surveyed included a peer support component. The "peer counseling" activities usually involved student-to-student tasks designed to identify, stabilize, or refer troubled students. These programs recommended instructing peer counselors in befriending, listening, identification, and referral skills. Approximately half of the training programs for peers were taught by school personnel and approximately half by outside mental health professionals. Seventy-three percent of the programs surveyed included crisis intervention components for dealing with the aftermath of suicide or a suicide attempt. Most programs included a crisis management team of four to seven individuals, who were given specialized training. These teams reported that the majority of their activities in a crisis situation involved dealing with other students, especially those previously identified as being at risk. . . .

Standards Must Be Set

Because the liabilities and potential contributions of school-related suicide programs are so great, there is a significant need to develop standards for the content and supervision procedures of these programs. Beginning efforts are underway to develop standards for school-related suicide programs. The American Association of Suicidology appointed a 26-member task force to develop a model for suicide prevention programs in the nation's public schools. This task force, composed of eminent suicidologists, educators, and researchers, met in a working session in 1987 at what has come to be called the Wingspread Conference. The final report of this task force will provide guidelines which should be helpful in both establishing and reviewing suicide prevention programs in the public schools.

It is important that school personnel not become overly discouraged by criticisms of current practice. As P. Cantor explained, we are in a crisis situation and our young people cannot wait. Progress has been made, in that some help is available where none existed 10 years ago. However, it is now time to refine our procedures through research, for this will lead to intervention strategies better able to achieve desired outcome goals.

The Important Role of Parents

Parents have been largely overlooked as a potential resource for suicide prevention in the past. Parents can help both as educators and by becoming educated. Survivors of Suicide (SOS) groups, many of whom are parents, have been organized in cities across the United States. Generally, members of these groups are willing to share their first-hand experience of suicide with other groups. Parent-Teacher Association (PTA) meetings are excellent opportunities for educating both parents and teachers about the realities of suicide and the methods of coping with suicidal behavior. Such programs ideally should be done by authorities in a well-planned series rather than one 30- to 60-minute session; this will ensure adequate time to discuss the complexities of child and adolescent suicide and give parents a chance to digest material and to raise questions that occur to them between sessions. Informed parents are invaluable as supporters of suicide education programs in the schools and as members of crisis intervention teams.

"*Using the media to inform viewers . . . is one possible way to reach some of these potentially suicidal adolescents.*"

The Media Can Help Prevent Suicide

Alan L. Berman

Research shows that television, movies, and other forms of mass media have a profound effect on Americans. Alan L. Berman, the author of the following viewpoint, agrees and argues that the media should use this influence to help prevent suicide. Berman proposes that the media create public service announcements that educate the public about suicide. Berman is a psychology professor at American University in Washington, D.C.

As you read, consider the following questions:

1. What is the relationship between violence on television and violent behavior in children, according to the author?
2. List the characteristics of an effective public service announcement as given by the author.
3. How do publicized news stories of celebrity suicides affect adolescents, according to Berman?

Adapted from the Alcohol, Drug Abuse, and Mental Health Administration's *Report of the Secretary's Task Force on Youth Suicide, vol. 2: Mass Media and Youth Suicide Prevention* by Alan L. Berman. Washington, DC: U.S. Government Printing Office, 1989.

The stereotype of the mass media is that of an omnipotent sculptor of attitudes, interests, and behaviors of a highly malleable and responsive public. After all, if the advertising it presents can effectively merchandise products as diverse as detergents and politicians, then surely it must be responsible for stimulating and controlling the behavior of large numbers of people.

Social scientists who have investigated the effect of the mass media on human behavior have been primarily concerned with the impact (essentially negative) of television. Of special interest here are those studies suggesting media influences on aggressive—specifically suicidal—behavior among young people. If such a negative impact can be documented, then preventive efforts can focus on attenuating these effects.

Television and Youth

Among adolescents, television is the preeminent medium and a trusted source of information. There is clear evidence that television advertising aimed at the youth market is successful in influencing purchasing behavior. Television as a whole has been described as a significant source of socialization and, by the National Institute of Mental Health (NIMH) as "a significant part of the total acculturation process."

Estimates of viewing habits of adolescents, ranging from 18 to 21 hours to nearly 28 hours per week, have led to the observation that typical American youth spend more time watching TV than at any other single activity, including school. Among the more negative stimuli to which the typical young viewer is exposed during these hours are frequent depictions of people drinking alcohol and a barrage of violent images and acts.

Content analyses of television programming have found that alcohol use, both casual and heavy, occurs twice as often as the drinking of coffee or tea. B. Greenberg estimates that the average viewer who is too young to drink will see about 3,000 drinking acts per year, although L. Wallack et al. argue that heavy or irresponsible drinking is shown only infrequently. Similarly, very little licit or illicit drug use is depicted on television. In contrast, televised acts of violence have been described [by S. Huntley and H. Kennedy] as "so pervasive that, by graduation day, the average high-school student has seen 18,000 murders" and 800 suicides.

Violence on Television and Aggressive Behavior

The most widely publicized conclusion of the NIMH-sponsored review of the relevant scientific literature on television and behavior was that "violence on television does lead to aggressive behavior by children and teenagers who watch the pro-

Increase in U.S. Suicides After Suicide Stories Appear on the Front Page of *The New York Times*, 1957-67

Name of Publicized Suicide	Date of Suicide Story	Observed No. of Suicides in Mo. After Suicide Story	Expected No. of Suicides in Mo. After Suicide Story	Rise in No. of U.S. Suicides After Suicide Story
Norman (Canadian ambassador)	Apr. 5, 1957	1,511	1,649.5	-138.5
Young (financier)	Jan. 26, 1958	1,361	1,352	9.0
Schupler (N.Y.C. councilman)	May 3, 1958	1,672	1,587	85.0
Quiggle (admiral)	July 25, 1958	1,519	1,451	68.0
Zwillman (underworld leader)	Feb. 27, 1959	1,707	1,609	98.0
Bang-Jensen (U.N. diplomat)	Nov. 27, 1959	1,477	1,423	54.0
Smith (police chief)	Mar. 20, 1960	1,669	1,609	60.0
Gedik (Turkish minister)	May 31, 1960	1,568	1,628.5	-60.5
Monroe (film star)	Aug. 6, 1962	1,838	1,640.5	197.5
Ward (implicated in Profumo Affair)	Aug. 4, 1963	1,801	1,640.5	160.5
Heyde & Tillman (Nazi officials)	Feb. 14, 1964	1,647	1,584.5	62.5
Lord (N.J. party chief)	June 17, 1965	1,801	1,743	58.0
Burros (KKK leader)	Nov. 1, 1965	1,710	1,652	58.0
Morrison (war critic)	Nov. 3, 1965			
Mott (American in Russian jail)	Jan. 22, 1966	1,757	1,717	40.0
Pike (son of Bishop Pike)	Feb. 5, 1966	1,620	1,567.5	52.5
Kravchenko (Russian defector)	Feb. 26, 1966	1,921	1,853	68.0
LoJui-Ching (Chinese army leader)	Jan. 21, 1967	1,821	1,717	104.0
Amer (Egyptian field marshal)	Sept. 16, 1967	1,770	1,733.5	36.5
Total				1,298.5

Source: David P. Phillips, (1974), The influence of suggestion on suicide, *American Sociological Review*, 39:344.

grams." Although the link was not seen as enduring, it was described as "causal." The researchers proposed several theories, all of which are common to suicidology, to account for the observed effects: (a) observational learning (imitation and modeling), (b) disinhibition, (c) attitude change, (d) desensitization and heightened arousal, and (e) justification of preexisting aggressive behavior.

Representatives of the broadcast industry and others have questioned the evidence and conclusions presented in the government review and criticized the studies as methodologically inadequate and proving correlation but not causation. However, while noting that research never yields unequivocal interpretations, E.A. Rubinstein concluded that "the convergence of evidence from many studies (of television and aggression) is overwhelming."

Media and Imitative Suicide

If violence on television promotes imitative aggressive behavior, can it be demonstrated that media depictions of suicide promote suicidal behavior among its viewers? . . .

The effect of publicized suicides on imitative behavior has been most consistently documented in studies of the print media. In an early paper, D.P. Phillips found statistically significant increases in suicides just after front-page suicide stories. Phillips termed this phenomenon the "Werther effect," referring to an alleged rash of imitative youth suicides that followed the publication of Goethe's *The Sorrows of Young Werther* in 1774. Phillips showed that the Werther effect increased proportionally to the amount of publicity devoted to the suicide and that it occurred primarily in the geographic area where the suicide story was published. I. Wasserman extended Phillips' data set and reexamined his findings. His analysis revealed that only stories of celebrity suicides appeared to elicit imitative behavior. Recently, S. Stack reported an extension of this work, demonstrating that entertainers had a more significant effect on imitative suicides than other celebrities (e.g., politicians, criminals) and that this effect on suicide rates was as profound as that found for unemployment. Moreover, Stack demonstrated that the effect was specific to those in a similar social role—stories of young male suicides most affected suicides of young males.

Other work by Phillips has linked publicized suicides to transient increases in other forms of violent death that might serve to disguise suicidal intent, namely, motor vehicle accidents and noncommercial airplane crashes.

L. Davidson and M. Gould have summarized this research and concluded that nonfictional, media-reported suicides do serve as models for imitative behavior. The evidence linking fictional models with imitative behavior is, however, more controversial and less conclusive.

Imitating Fiction

Anecdotal reports of imitative suicide following presentations of fictional suicides on television and in movies have appeared. T. Radecki has documented 37 deaths by Russian roulette worldwide between 1978 and April, 1985 attributed to imitations initiated by viewing the movie "The Deer Hunter." Even rock music has been blamed for stimulating suicide. Until recently, however, no one had presented empirical evidence for a relationship between fictional suicides and imitative suicide.

Gould and Davidson have reported the first such data. They examined completed youth suicides for metropolitan New York City, southwestern Connecticut, and all of New Jersey as well as admissions at six New York area hospitals for attempts two weeks before and two weeks after each of four televised movies presenting fictional suicides. They found significant increases in both attempts and completions in the followup period. . . .

Mass Media and Prevention

One approach to the prevention of youth suicide is to limit or inhibit stimulating influences on suicidal behavior. To the extent that the media may present models for imitation or where the media depicts behaviors that predispose depressogenic conditions (e.g., makes alcohol consumption seem attractive), then reducing these influences would be appropriate.

However, the media may also take a more active and positive role in prevention. Educating the populace could increase early detection of potentially suicidal youth. Using the media to inform viewers about health problems and to provide models that promote health-conscious behavior is one possible way to reach some of these potentially suicidal adolescents and thus reduce the population at risk.

Public Service Announcements

Public service announcements (PSAs) are the most typical mass media vehicle for campaigns to educate the public and promote health. PSAs attempt to increase viewers' awareness of a specific problem and possible solutions. In addition, some aim at changing beliefs, attitudes, motivations, and behaviors; however, significant change generally fails to occur. . . .

B.R. Flay and H.K. Goldstein have suggested several guidelines for effective PSA campaigns. PSAs should be novel and use a knowledgeable, credible spokesperson with whom the audience can identify. The content of the PSA should be based on scientific fact and delivered in a manner that minimizes the arousal of fear. Also, clear alternative behaviors should be presented. The PSA needs widespread dissemination, high saturation (frequent exposure), and extended duration of exposure. To be most effective, PSAs need to be supplemented by other media (e.g., print) and community networking. PSAs have been developed that focus on suicide prevention. Highly professional PSAs have been produced by and are available from the Los Angeles Suicide Prevention Center and the American Association of Suicidology. However, to date, no evaluation of their effectiveness has been conducted. . . .

Historically, mass media public information campaigns have rested on the assumption that problems should be addressed with more and better information. Thus, information has been confused with education, and education with prevention. Behavior change does not result from mere exposure to well-designed informational messages. This "hypodermic needle theory" is too simplistic and has not been proven to be effective.

Effective suicide prevention must rest on the assumption that the target group—those at risk (potentially suicidal adolescents) or those around the person at risk (parents, teachers, peers)—can be reached by, will attend to, participate in, and respond to preventive messages. The messages must be informational (e.g., signs and symptoms, cues) and directional (e.g., where to get help); but, also, they must provide skills and incentives to act.

How do you get high risk adolescents, those who are acting out, depressed, abusing substances, etc., to pay attention to suicide prevention programming? What have we learned from studying mass media prevention efforts that increases the likelihood of having positive impact?

V.F. Sacco and R.A. Silverman have outlined five principles, inferred from empirical data, for successful mass media prevention campaigns: (a) information must be readily available to the target audience, (b) communication strategies must be designed to be salient to multiple targets, (c) contradictory information must be minimized, (d) objectives must be realistic and specific, and (e) desired behaviors to be pursued by the audience must be made explicit.

B.R. Flay and J.L. Sobel suggest that mass media efforts must use multiple sources of information, extend campaigns over time, and convince gatekeepers (e.g., television station managers) of the worth of the campaign, to ensure adequate dissemination. They argue that more persons will pay attention if the message is seen as meeting a salient need (e.g., offers a skill) and is delivered by someone with whom adolescents identify or on whom they model themselves (e.g., music groups, sports figures). Furthermore, and perhaps most important, they contend that media programs must be both complemented and supplemented by school-based curricula, home/family involvement, or community organization designed to increase interpersonal communication, discussion and networking.

Interpersonal Communication Is Vital

The most successfully designed mass media campaigns that promote changes in health behavior are those that incorporate interpersonal communication. For example, the USC/KABC-TV

Smoking Prevention and Cessation Program consisted of five 5-minute news segments, a coordinated 5-day classroom curriculum for junior high students emphasizing social skills regarding resisting social influence, homework assignments requiring adult involvement, a followup series of five 5-minute news segments, and a written guide provided to all parents. Students involved in the program made significant gains in smoking cessation and non-initiation.

The Profound Effect of Movies

Madelyn Gould and David Shaffer of Columbia University researched the effect of four made-for-TV movies about teenage suicide broadcast over a six-month period in late 1984 and early 1985. Teenage suicide rates in the Metropolitan New York area rose in the two weeks after three of the four movies were broadcast; six more teenagers than would have been expected took their lives. Attempted suicides rose by 40 percent. . . . Psychiatrist Leon Eisenberg wrote, "It is timely to ask whether there are measures that should be undertaken to limit media coverage of suicide."

George Howe Colt, *The Enigma of Suicide*, 1991.

To teach specific behavioral skills, the Stanford Heart Disease Three Community Study included intensive mass media campaigns (PSAs, radio and television features, newspaper articles, bus cards, billboards) and face-to-face clinics for high risk subjects. The program extended over two years and significantly reduced risk for cardiovascular disease.

The Crime Prevention Coalition, with the cooperation of the Advertising Council, produced the national "Take a Bite Out of Crime" campaign. This program relied heavily on well-produced PSAs designed to induce behavioral change, a coordinated print campaign, and local community projects. Significant changes were accomplished in six of seven target goals.

A similar and impressively coordinated effort, has been mounted by WQED-TV in Pittsburgh. "The Chemical People" project involved two PBS television shows, educational print resources, and guides. Most importantly, it involved citizen outreach activities which resulted in more than 10,000 town meetings which evolved into continuing task forces to deal with youth drug problems on a community level.

The mass media are not responsible for causing youth suicide nor are they responsible for preventing youth suicide. Yet, as a significant part of the sociocultural milieu in which our children are raised, they have the potential to profoundly alter the message environment in which children behave.

To the extent that publicized news stories about celebrity suicides contribute to the suicide of a youngster predisposed to suicide, concern within the media needs to be raised. Newsworthiness is an appropriate consideration in the amount and type of coverage given a news event. Celebrity suicides are newsworthy, but the possibility of imitative suicides as a consequence to their reports suggests some balance needs to be considered. Neither censorship nor prior restraint are appropriate, but limits may be. Elective guidelines might be established. Consultative discussion between media representatives and suicidologists might, for example, achieve some desired balance between the public's need to know, the media's right to report, and alternative consequences. To the extent that the media may be used to educate, concentrating on prosocial education in early childhood appears to be the best possible use of the media for prevention. To the extent that children can be influenced by positive models, taught instrumental skills, etc., and to the extent that positive models are presented by the media, there is likely to be some lessening of the multitude of factors that lead to suicidal behavior.

VIEWPOINT

"The goals for suicide prevention . . . would be
first to increase the social integration and social
regulation of people."

Changes in Society Can Help Prevent Suicide

David Lester

David Lester is a psychology professor at Richard Stockton State
College in Pomona, New Jersey, and the author of several books
on suicide, including *Understanding and Preventing Suicide*, from
which the following viewpoint is excerpted. In the viewpoint,
Lester states that many people commit suicide because they feel
alienated from society—they have no close relationships with
friends or family members. Lester proposes that increasing
these social ties could help prevent suicide. He suggests that society work to reach out to the lonely and alienated, and make
them feel that they belong to the community.

As you read, consider the following questions:

1. What two theories did Emile Durkheim propose concerning
   suicide, according to Lester?
2. What role does self-esteem play in suicide, in the author's
   opinion?
3. Why does Lester believe suicidal patients benefit more from
   group therapy than from individual therapy?

From David Lester, *Understanding and Preventing Suicide*, 1990. Courtesy of Charles C
Thomas, Publisher, Springfield, Illinois.

The first major theory of suicide was proposed by Emile Durkheim (1897), who argued that suicide was caused by two social forces. *Social integration* referred to the degree to which individuals in the society were bound by social ties and relationships, while *social regulation* referred to the degree to which individuals had their desires and emotions controlled by the social values of the society. Durkheim held that suicide would be more likely if social integration was too weak (leading to egoistic suicide), if social regulation was too weak (leading to anomic suicide), or if these two social forces were too strong (leading to altruistic and fatalistic suicide, respectively).

B.D. Johnson (1965) noted that Durkheim both defined four types of suicide and made predictions about which social conditions led to high rates of suicide. Although altruistic and fatalistic make good sense as types of suicide, they are relatively rare. So Johnson proposed modifying Durkheim's theory, predicting that suicide would be more common if social integration and social regulation were weak.

It can be seen readily that Durkheim's theory focuses upon the social bond between the individual and society and so fits into social control theory. As a sociologist, Durkheim was not interested in the factors affecting the development of social integration and social regulation. However, he did point to a number of social processes that affected the strength of these two social forces, such as marriage versus divorce and religious affiliation. . . .

The Psychological Level

(1) *The social bond.* It has long been known that suicide rates are highest among the divorced and the widowed and lowest for those who are married. Completed suicide may also be less common among people who have children. S. Ganzler (1967) found that attempted suicides were experiencing greater social isolation than psychiatrically disturbed but non-suicidal patients. Furthermore, both Lester (1969) and Ganzler (1967) found that suicidal individuals rated their significant others more negatively than did non-suicidal individuals.

Lester's (1983) review of the literature found consistent evidence that suicidal individuals came from more disorganized homes and felt less close to their parents than non-suicidal individuals.

Perhaps the most comprehensive study of the degree to which child-parent bonds are disrupted in suicidal individuals was a study conducted by J. Jacobs (1971) on adolescent suicide attempters. He found that the adolescent suicide attempters had not merely experienced a broken home, for example, but that there was a long-standing history of problems in their families of which the broken home was but one incident. The parents of the suicidal adolescent were more likely to remarry and subsequently divorce than the parents of the non-suicidal teenagers. The parents of the suicidal adolescents were more likely to nag, yell and physically punish their children, and their children felt more alienated.

C. Thomas and K. Duszynski (1974) compared medical students who committed suicide later in their lives with those who did not and found that the suicides more often reported having emotionally undemonstrative parents and having felt less close to their parents.

Self-Esteem and Suicide

(2) *Ego strength*. Several studies have reported low self-esteem in suicidal individuals. For example, C. Neuringer (1974) found that attempted suicides rated themselves as more negatively and others as more positively than did psychosomatic patients. H. Kaplan and A.D. Pokorny (1976) found that low self-esteem predicted subsequent suicidal ideation and suicidal attempts in seventh-grade children.

Number of Close Friends Subject Had in the Last Year Before Suicide Attempt or Death

Number of Close Friends	Natural Deaths	Suicide Attempters	Suicide Completers
0	33%	22%	49%
1	11%	11%	18%
2	13%	27%	11%
3 +	29%	35%	11%
Unknown	14%	5%	11%
Total	100%	100%	100%

Source: Ronald W. Maris, *Pathways to Suicide*. Baltimore, MD: The Johns Hopkins University Press, 1981, p. 115.

These reports of low self-esteem in suicidal individuals are consistent with reports of the high levels of depression and feelings of hopelessness in suicidal individuals.

Psychologists consider that perceiving yourself as responsible for both the good and the bad things that happen to you is a sign of psychological health. There is some evidence that suicidal people tend more often than non-suicidal people to have a belief in an external locus of control, that is, to believe that what happens to them is mainly due to chance or the influence of other people rather than as a result of what they themselves do. A recent study reported, for example, that current suicidal ideation in college students was associated with belief in an external locus of control, even after controlling for the level of depression.

Increased Impulsiveness

Many authors have commented on impulsiveness in suicidal individuals. For example, B. Corder et al. (1974) found that adolescent suicide attempters were generally more impulsive and active than non-suicidal adolescents. Recently, Lester (1990) found that college students who had threatened suicide scored higher on a test of general impulsivity than equally depressed but non-suicidal college students. L. Epstein et al. (1973) found that medical students who subsequently committed suicide later in their lives were rated as more impulsive while in medical school.

It can be seen that a strong case can be made for a social control theory of suicide. Most of the sociological theorizing about suicide is really based on social controls, and a good deal of psychological research has pointed to the influence of poor relationships with parents, conflicts with lovers and friends, and social isolation on the development and appearance of suicidal behavior.

Suicidal people also appear to be deficient in internal controls. They have poor self-images and are seriously depressed, tend to be impulsive, and prone to blame others for their misfortunes.

Implications for Suicide Prevention

The goals for suicide prevention in this perspective would be first to increase the social integration and social regulation of people. The society needs to discourage those actions which decrease social integration and regulation, such as divorce, and encourage those actions which increase social integration and regulation, such as church affiliation and social networking.

Those working in communities need to find ways to increase the social bonding for particular groups in society. Activities such as athletic leagues for kids and exercise and social groups for the elderly can provide primary prevention of alienation and anomie in a society. Interestingly some of the recent activities by city residents to drive drug dealers off their streets serve this function well. The residents on a street band together with a common goal and organize activities around this goal. These activities often include cleaning up the streets and actively being out on and socializing in the streets so that the drug dealers and purchasers find it easier to move elsewhere to conduct their transactions. Some cities have organized elections for street and block leaders to organize block parties and to beautify the city.

Society and Suicide

Suicide varies inversely with the degree of integration of the social groups of which the individual forms a part. . . .

When society is strongly integrated, it holds individuals under its control, considers them at its service and thus forbids them to dispose wilfully of themselves. Accordingly it opposes their evading their duties to it through death. But how could society impose its supremacy upon them when they refuse to accept this subordination as legitimate? It no longer then possesses the requisite authority to retain them in their duty if they wish to desert; and conscious of its own weakness, it even recognizes their right to do freely what it can no longer prevent. So far as they are the admitted masters of their destinies, it is their privilege to end their lives. They, on their part, have no reason to endure life's sufferings patiently. For they cling to life more resolutely when belonging to a group they love, so as not to betray interests they put before their own. The bond that unites them with the common cause attaches them to life and the lofty goal they envisage prevents their feeling personal troubles so deeply. There is, in short, in a cohesive and animated society a constant interchange of ideas and feelings from all to each and each to all, something like a mutual moral support, which instead of throwing the individual on his own resources, leads him to share in the collective energy and supports his own when exhausted.

Emile Durkheim, *Suicide*, [1897], 1951.

It is worth noting that often these types of activities are typically organized to combat a problem other than suicide and that they are often organized by religious and other activist groups. It does not seem likely that suicide prevention would ever serve as the stimulus for such activities, but suicide prevention may result incidentally from these action programs.

School Programs

Suicide prevention, along with the prevention of other disturbed and unproductive behaviors, can be facilitated by the development of schools which are attractive to children. Schools must provide good role models in their teachers and must bond the children to the school by making school an interesting and pleasant place to be, goals which need not interfere with the educational functions.

Too many school teachers are incompetent. They are mediocre

students graduating from state colleges who are unqualified for better positions. Too much of their time is taken up with discipline and keeping order in classes which are too large. Teachers need to work more closely with smaller numbers of students, making learning exciting and interesting and demonstrating this by their own attitude to life.

Two examples of recent successful programs along these lines were given by S. Tifft (1990). One program set up classes for young black boys with no fathers at home. Attendance and academic performance improved and hostility decreased, but the program was halted because it violated civil rights laws. Another program has recruited black male professionals to come into the schools to work with children of both sexes. These are the types of programs which schools must offer, and not simply as special programs, but rather as part of the everyday routine of teaching and designed for all types of students.

The Family

Although it has long been accepted that we live in social groups and that psychotherapy with these larger groups might be more effective than working with individuals, family therapy has always been inhibited by the fact that many of those in a social group refuse to accept the need for therapy. The parents, brothers and sisters, and children of a disturbed individual often simply want the psychotherapist to take the disturbed individual and "cure" him or her. Getting them to be willing to participate, let alone be enthusiastic about participating, in family therapy is extremely difficult. Even when a family is motivated to come to family therapy, the motivation of some members decreases rapidly as the first signs of improvement appear.

However, the social control perspective requires that the bonds between the depressed and potentially suicidal individual and his or her family need to be developed and maintained in a psychological healthy style. Joseph Richman (1986) has recently written the first book dealing with the family treatment of suicidal individuals, and we must hope that this style of therapy becomes more and more common in the future.

Psychotherapy

Since some of the social controls against suicide must be internal, psychotherapy would seem useful in building a positive self-image, a strong ego, high frustration tolerance, and goal orientation. However, psychotherapy is going to affect only a small percentage of the population who might benefit from it.

Most individuals in a suicidal crisis who contact a mental health agency visit a suicide prevention and crisis service or a community mental health facility. These agencies typically use crisis intervention techniques often with a paraprofessional counselor. Crisis counseling is not designed for achieving the goals listed above.

In rare cases, agencies may operate groups for suicidal patients. Because of the usefulness of increasing the social bonding of depressed and suicidal clients, group therapy may be preferable to individual psychotherapy for these clients, since social bonding is one of the major results of group psychotherapy. However, group therapy run by professional therapists imposes limits on the clients, such as no social contact outside of the group and no romantic involvements between group members.

Given the ideas suggested by the social control perspective, it would seem useful to provide social network groups for depressed and suicidal people in addition to therapy groups, that is, groups whose function would be to help structure the time and activities of the clients outside of therapy hours. These social network groups could arrange evening meals, visits to movies, and other activities which would help bond the depressed and suicidal individuals to others in the social group.

The limitations of psychotherapy, either individual or group, are fine for clients who are not facing the decision of whether to commit suicide. However, for potentially suicidal clients more social support must be provided in addition to the psychotherapeutic experiences.

"If someone you know is suicidal . . . your willingness to do something about it could make the difference between life and death."

Intervention by Friends Can Help Prevent Suicide

Suicide Prevention and Crisis Center of San Mateo County, California

In the following viewpoint, the authors give guidelines that can be followed to help friends and family members avoid suicide. The authors believe that people who understand the danger signs can better talk to and prevent a friend from committing suicide. The San Mateo County Suicide Prevention and Crisis Center works to educate citizens about suicide and to offer counseling to those in crisis and to those contemplating suicide.

As you read, consider the following questions:

1. What danger signs of suicide do the authors list?
2. Why is it important to discuss suicide with those who might be suicidal, according to the authors?
3. What resources can provide help to suicidal people, according to the authors?

Adapted, with permission, from *Suicide in Youth and What You Can Do About It—A Guide for Students*, prepared by the Suicide Prevention and Crisis Center of San Mateo County, California.

What would you do if one of your friends threatened to commit suicide?

Would you laugh it off?

Would you assume that the threat was just a joke or a way of getting attention?

Would you be shocked and tell him or her not to say things like that?

Would you ignore it?

If you reacted in any of those ways you might be missing an opportunity to save a life, perhaps the life of someone who is very close and important to you. You might later find yourself saying, "I didn't believe she was serious," or "I never thought he'd really do it."

Suicide is a major cause of death. The American Association of Suicidology estimates that it claims 35,000 lives each year in the United States alone; some authorities feel that the true figure may be closer to 100,000. A growing number of those lives are young people in their teens and early twenties. Although it is difficult to get an accurate count because many suicides are covered up or reported as accidents, suicide is now thought to be the second leading cause of death among young people.

If someone you know is suicidal, your ability to recognize the signs and your willingness to do something about it could make the difference between life and death.

Danger Signs

No doubt you have heard that people who talk about suicide won't really do it. It isn't true. Before committing suicide, people often make direct statements about their intention to end their lives, or less direct comments about how they might as well be dead or that their friends and family would be better off without them. Suicide threats and similar statements should always be taken seriously. They are a very real sign of danger.

People who have tried to kill themselves before, even if their attempts didn't seem very serious, are also at risk. Unless they are helped they may try again, and the next time the result might be fatal. Four out of five persons who commit suicide have made at least one previous attempt.

Perhaps someone you know has suddenly begun to act very differently or seems to have taken on a whole new personality. The shy person becomes a thrill-seeker. The outgoing person becomes withdrawn, unfriendly and disinterested. When such changes take place for no apparent reason or persist for a period of time, it may be a clue to impending suicide.

Making final arrangements is another possible indication of suicidal risk. In young people, such arrangements often include giving away treasured personal possessions, such as a favorite book, record or collection.

If someone confides in you that he or she is thinking about suicide or shows other signs of being suicidal, don't be afraid to talk about it. Your willingness to discuss it will show the person that you don't condemn him or her for having such feelings. Ask questions about how the person feels and about the reasons for those feelings.

Suicide Facts and Myths

1. Fable: People who talk about suicide don't commit suicide.

   Fact: Of any 10 persons who kill themselves, 8 have given definite warnings of their suicidal intentions.

2. Fable: Suicide happens without warning.

   Fact: Suicidal people give many clues and warnings regarding their suicidal intentions.

3. Fable: Suicidal people are fully intent on dying.

   Fact: Most suicidal people are undecided about living or dying, and they "gamble with death," leaving it to others to save them.

4. Fable: Improvement following a suicidal crisis means that the suicidal risk is over.

   Fact: Most suicides occur within about three months following the beginning of "improvement," when individuals have the energy to put their morbid thoughts and feelings into effect.

5. Fable: Suicide is inherited.

   Fact: Suicide does not run in families. It is an individual pattern.

6. Fable: All suicidal individuals are mentally ill.

   Fact: Although suicidal people are extremely unhappy, they are not necessarily mentally ill.

Source: Edwin Shneidman, 1952.

Ask whether a method of suicide has been considered, whether any specific plans have been made and whether any steps have been taken toward carrying out those plans, such as getting hold of whatever means of suicide has been decided upon.

Don't worry that your discussion will encourage the person to go through the plan. On the contrary, it will help him or her to know that someone is willing to be a friend. It may save a life.

On the other hand, don't try to turn the discussion off or offer advice such as, "Think about how much better off you are than most people. You should appreciate how lucky you are." Such comments only make the suicidal person feel more guilty, worthless and hopeless than before. Be a concerned and willing listener. Keep calm. Discuss the subject as you would any other topic of concern with a friend.

Get Help

Whenever you think that someone you know is in danger of suicide, get help. Suggest that he or she call a suicide prevention center, crisis intervention center or whatever similar organization serves your area. Or suggest that they talk with a sympathetic teacher, counselor, clergyman, doctor or other adult you respect. If your friend refuses, take it upon yourself to talk with one of these people for advice on handling the situation.

In some cases you may find yourself in the position of having to get direct help for someone who is suicidal and refuses to go for counseling. If so, do it. Don't be afraid of appearing disloyal. Many people who are suicidal have given up hope. They no longer believe they can be helped. They feel it is useless. The truth is, they *can* be helped. With time, most suicidal people can be restored to full and happy living. But when they are feeling hopeless, their judgment is impaired. They can't see a reason to go on living. In that case, it is up to you to use *your* judgment to see that they get the help they need. What at the time may appear to be an act of disloyalty or the breaking of a confidence could turn out to be the favor of a lifetime. Your courage and willingness to act could save a life.

What About You?

Perhaps you have sometimes felt like ending your life. Don't be ashamed of it. Many people, young and old, share your feelings. Talk to someone you trust. If you like, you can call one of the agencies mentioned above and talk about the way you feel without telling them who you are. Things seem very bad sometimes. But those times don't last forever. Ask for help. You *can* be helped. Because you deserve it.

"Suicide prevention in the elderly relates to improving the self-esteem of older persons. "

Improving the Lives of the Elderly Can Prevent Suicide

Alexander C. Morgan

The elderly have the highest suicide rate of any age group in the United States. In the following viewpoint, Alexander C. Morgan attributes this high rate of suicide to many factors, including depression, poor health, and poverty, which afflict many of the elderly. Morgan believes that changing the lives of elderly Americans—helping them feel valuable and improving their health care and economic status—could prevent suicide among the elderly. Morgan is an instructor in psychiatry at Harvard Medical School in Cambridge, Massachusetts, and the former medical director of geriatric services at Cambridge Hospital.

As you read, consider the following questions:

1. What group among the elderly has the highest suicide rate, according to the author?
2. Why does Morgan believe it is important that elderly suicidal people be provided with a number of caregivers?
3. What is the most important aspect of caring for the elderly, in Morgan's opinion?

From Alexander C. Morgan, "Special Issues of Assessment and Treatment of Suicide Risk in the Elderly," in *Suicide: Understanding and Responding*, Douglas Jacobs and Herbert N. Brown, eds. Madison, CT: International Universities Press, 1989. Copyright 1989 by Douglas Jacobs and Herbert N. Brown. Reprinted with permission.

At 6:30 a.m. the night nurse in a reputable nursing home found 79-year-old Mr. Delgado dead in his bed with a gunshot wound of the head inflicted by a pistol he held in his right hand. No one had known Mr. Delgado to be mentally ill, and at the time of his death his only active physical illness was a 24-hour-long, severe, unremitting case of diarrhea, which had caused him the unusual embarrassment of soiling his bed. Mr. Delgado had been rather isolated and irritable throughout the four years he had been in the nursing home, but the nursing home psychiatrist had never been asked to consult regarding him. The most notable aspect about his time in the nursing home was that he had vehemently refused to let anyone help him remove the prosthetic leg he wore after an amputation due to a gunshot wound to that leg 30 years previously. It was in that prosthesis that the gun had been kept all this time.

The startling features of the above case highlight the difficulties in assessing and treating suicide risk in the elderly. The combination of social isolation and drastically experienced physical illness must have given Mr. Delgado a sense of hopelessness that eventually overwhelmed him. Additionally, the extreme lethality of his method of suicide made intervention impossible for the health care personnel working with him. The social isolation, physical illness, and highly lethal attempt are some of the factors that will be reviewed as requiring special attention in assessing suicide risk in the elderly. The emphasis will be on the special clinical problems confronted in assessing and treating elderly suicide risk. . . .

Overview of the Elderly Suicide Rate

Perhaps the best known fact about suicide among the elderly in the United States is that the rate in this age group is higher than at any other time in the life cycle. Figure 1 shows that the suicide rate rises to its highest point in the 75- to 79-year age group. While increased age is an important determinant of suicide risk, sex and race are probably more telling, with the male suicide rate continuing to climb with advancing age, but the female suicide rate leveling off at 65. Also, whites historically have had higher rates of suicide than nonwhites. Thus, the older white males have the highest risk.

While the high rate of elderly suicide is alarming relative to other causes of death in this age group, death by suicide is not as common a cause of death as it is at other ages. Heart disease, malignancies, and cerebrovascular diseases are only a few causes of death in the elderly that are more common than suicide. In many ways, suicide risk is a more treatable potential cause of death than the more common potential causes of death in the elderly such as heart disease, cancer, and so on. The fact that suicide is less common than other causes of death in the elderly, however, may influence people working with them to be inattentive to elderly suicide risk.

An additional, clinically meaningful statistic to be considered in working with elderly potential suicides is that it appears that those elderly who attempt suicide succeed more often than persons attempting suicide in the younger age groups. The means of suicide chosen by the elderly is also more violent and lethal (hanging, drowning, gunshot wound). These findings, coupled with the old saw that suicide is a permanent solution for a temporary problem, are in fact the strongest arguments for suicide risk detection and assessment in the elderly.

Suicide Rates by Age Group

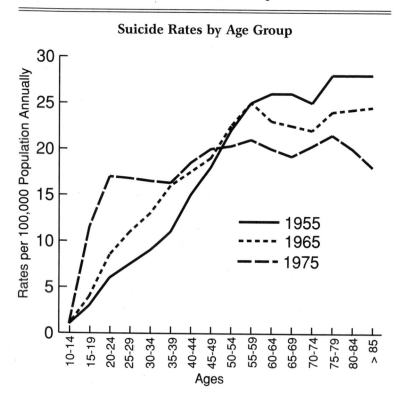

Source: C. Fredericks, *American Journal of Psychotherapy*, 1978.

Before leaving the subject of suicide rate statistics in the United States, it is important to note that the U.S. pattern of a higher suicide rate in the older population is not universal, though it probably is the most common. For instance, statistics for Finland show that the suicide rate for males peaks at age 50 and then declines, in contrast to the statistics for U.S. males. In comparing rates from a variety of countries there is the general, though not definitive, impression that societies in which the elderly hold a more valued position have lower rates of elderly suicide. One clear validation of this phenomenon was studied in Hong Kong when the elderly suicide rate in 1922 was compared to rates in 1950 and found to be substantially lower. In the three decades between the two sets of statistics the older Hong Kong citizens had lost some of their social-cultural prominence due to changes away from the traditional reverence toward the elderly.

There has, interestingly, been a small decrease in the elderly suicide rate in the United States over the last 20 years, and some studies have shown that this regression can be almost entirely explained by the increase that has occurred in the level of elderly income over this time period. These data underscore a point that will become more clear in the course of discussing the treatment of elderly suicide risk: close attention must be paid to socioeconomic factors in the treatment of such patients. . . .

Mental Illness and Emotional State

Hopelessness is the most common feeling state of older persons committing suicide, and it often includes the sense that there is absolutely no other resolution to the suffering that the person faces. Diagnostically, depression, alcoholism, and organic brain syndrome are the most common mental disorders of the suicidal elderly population. However, depression is by far the most common, ranging from 48 to 80 percent of elderly suicides. In a cross-section of the elderly, primary depression was present in only 3.7 percent, with a total of 14 percent complaining of some kind of dysphoric state. The high percentage of elderly suicides who were depressed is in sharp contrast to the low of 3.7 percent of depression in the general population of the elderly, giving clear testimony to the fact that depression is a primary feature of elderly suicide. . . .

Physical Illnesses

A large percentage of people over 65 have chronic illnesses, so that it is not surprising that a high proportion (50 to 60 percent) of elderly suicides are reported to have physical illnesses. However, what seems to be more clinically significant is the psychological meaning of the physical illness to the older person. If the illness is seen as a direct blow to the person's means of maintaining self-esteem, such as the unremitting diarrhea for Mr. Delgado described in the introductory vignette, then there is indeed an increase of suicide risk.

There is some uncertainty as to the exact impact social and economic class have on the elderly suicide rate. However, it is abundantly clear that a negative change in socioeconomic class is associated with an increased risk of suicide. As with physical illnesses, it appears that it is the meaning of the socioeconomic variable to the individual person that causes increased risk. In the Great Depression of the 1930s the increased risk of suicide was largely in classes that lost a great deal of money rather than among people who were already moderately poor prior to the Depression. The difficulties of continuing on a fixed income in the face of inflation are very much part of some older people's despair about themselves. Other social factors associated with loss such as death of a spouse, retirement, and sense of isolation are also correlated with higher rates of suicide in some studies. It very much depends on the meaning of the specific sociocultural factor to the individual person. For instance, elderly widows do have a slightly higher suicide risk (increased 1.3 times) after the husband's death. However, this rise in suicide rate is less than the rise for younger widows. This implies that as women age there is an increase in their ability to tolerate their husband's death, and this finding perhaps bears upon age-related changes in women's social support network. The true importance of social variables in suicide evaluation of the elderly probably lies in the extent to which the elderly person feels integrated into the society to which he or she belongs. . . .

Treatment of Suicide Risk in the Elderly

The treatment of suicide risk in the elderly does not differ substantially from suicide treatment of other age groups. The prime issue at all ages is to increase the safety of the patient. Any substantial risk in an older person means that they should be hospitalized in a psychiatric unit. Because of physical problems, there may be an inclination to hospitalize elderly people on regular medical units. It may represent some wish of the caregivers to deny the emotional distress presented by the suicidal thinking. This is not in fact a reasonable solution for the emotional aspects of the suicide risk.

After the person's safety has been assured, the treatment must aim at decreasing the hopelessness of the patient. The depression that lies behind the hopeless feeling should be aggressively treated, because it is usually the depression that prevents the person from seeing the alternatives to suicide. The life-saving factor in suicide treatment is often the meaningful presence of a real working therapeutic alliance, or, in other words, a "confidante." With this relationship, the painful feelings behind the depression may be able to be tolerated in such a way as to help the patient feel worthy of staying alive. The full treatment regimen for depression should of course be used with depressed suicidal elderly. . . .

With suicidal elderly people the cause of the patient's depression almost always has some relationship to the realities of his or her life. Thus treatment should include "real" help when it is called for. Physical illness should be aggressively treated. Attention should be paid to maintaining the person's social surroundings as much as possible. Hospitalizations, especially psychiatric ones, often result in friends and relatives distancing themselves from the hospitalized patient. This is particularly true with elderly people and must be countered. In fact, there should be strong efforts to increase the number and availability of people involved with the patient. Family members, neighbors, visiting nurses, homemakers, welfare workers, day care center staff, medical care personnel such as the family doctor and his nurse, should all be involved both in helping the patient and also in communication to each other the status of their individual work with the patient. The patient should be encouraged to allow this kind of open communication between the caregivers. The intersystemic connection between the multitude of caregivers usually involved with the elderly is particularly important in preventing individual caregivers from feeling unnecessarily responsible and burdened by the patient and then withdrawing their availability for the patient. In increasing the contact between the patient and the people available to him, it is important that the contact be concrete and reality oriented when appropriate. Help with housekeeping and other daytime activities such as shopping may be as necessary as psychotropic medication in helping elderly patients regain their sense of self-worth and ability to manage their lives.

Committed to Suicide

Suicide among elderly people is a major problem in our society. They have the highest suicide rate of any age group. It has been estimated that each year as many as 10,000 deaths among the elderly may be the result of suicide. Elderly people are quite serious and strongly committed to suicide once a self-destructive decision is made. The old do not make suicidal gestures; their ratio of suicide completions to attempts is the highest of any age group.

Judith M. Stillion, Eugene E. McDowell, and Jacque H. May, *Suicide Across the Life Span*, 1989.

The contact with a suicidal elderly person should, from the beginning, incorporate as much continuity as possible. There are two periods of increased suicidal risk that occur in all ages but can be particularly dramatic with the elderly. The first period is just as help is beginning to be organized for the patient. Thus, it is important that, as soon as the decision has been made to provide assistance to the elderly person, there be no time when the patient could change his mind and successfully kill himself. The second period of increased risk takes place during the course of the treatment of the patient's depression, when the energy level has begun to rise but the patient's mood is still one of despair. There is at that time sufficient energy to go through with a suicide that the anergic state of the depression had previously prevented. With elderly patients there is a third period of high risk, though it is not so much an increase in risk as a dramatic return of the risk. That period occurs when, after a successful treatment and discharge from the hospital, the patient suffers some new, unanticipated blow to what maintains his self-esteem. This is true at all ages, of course, but the elderly person's financial, health, and social situation makes him more vulnerable to the usual inconsistencies of life. The failure to receive a Social Security check due to a bureaucratic oversight, the exacerbation of a chronic physical illness, or the closing of an elderly drop-in center can each have a serious negative effect on the elderly person's recovery from the despair that produced the suicidal thinking. For this reason, after-care planning for the elderly must be very comprehensive and must consider the large variety of supports the patient uses. The treatment must also be very responsive so that the support can be readily available if the feelings of hopelessness return.

Prevention of Elderly Suicide

Because of the high lethality of most elderly suicide attempts, the best treatment for elderly suicide risk is prevention. It will clearly be helpful if increased attention is paid to elderly people, both by clinicians and by society. There are particular problems, however, in that elderly people tend to underutilize suicide crisis centers. With the introduction of community mental health programs, there is mixed evidence about decreases in the elderly suicide rate, but the presence of outpatient treatment centers may have protected some elderly patients.

Primary prevention, that is, elimination of causes of illnesses, is really the most significant form of prevention of elderly suicide. Much of the suicidal thinking in the elderly arises after the individual experiences personal losses. Attempts at early detection and replacement of an older person's losses might have significant success in preventing the despair that produces suicidal thinking (though it is, of course, impossible to replace some losses, such as that of a spouse). However, if such an irremediable loss occurs and is detected, then other persons and services can at least make up for some of the feeling of deficit. At present the data about the success of such interventions show mixed results. Processes such as retirement preparation, widow-to-widow groups, or postfuneral follow-ups of mourners are the kind of social-psychological interventions that might have some impact on suicidal thinking following losses.

Essentially, suicide prevention in the elderly relates to improving the self-esteem of older persons and has wide social, financial, and political ramifications. While all depression and suicide thinking in the elderly is clearly not related to sociocultural issues, the demographics of elderly suicide show how important these factors truly are. Improving older persons' financial security, housing conditions, health care, and social isolation would have a real impact on their view of themselves within the society. Data have already been mentioned that show total statistical correlation between the slight decrease in the U.S. elderly suicide rate over the last three decades and the concurrent rise in elderly income separate from other social variables such as unemployment, divorce rates, and so on. With the well-publicized rising proportion of elderly in the United States population, improvement of older people's financial security is, of course, not without difficulty. However, more attention is now being paid to the condition of the nation's older citizens, including their high suicide rate. With this increased notice, it is becoming increasingly clear that it is necessary to develop improved ways of helping the growing number of elderly people maintain their feelings of self-worth within the society. . . .

A Final Word

The most important aspect of paying attention to older people is to see them as individuals. It is the intention of this viewpoint to draw attention to older people in general, and then as individuals. Older people are just as unique and varied, one from the other, as people at any other age. In short the message is first to begin to recognize that older people, and their heightened suicide risk, are very much present with us in our clinical work. After that, getting to know and appreciate the individual nature of each older person's own life story is no different from learning the life story of a person of any age. Because the older person's life story is, of course, longer, there may be added richness to the process of that clinical involvement with the elderly patient. It is hoped that readers will be encouraged to find out for themselves the special quality of the therapeutic relationship that develops when working with older patients.

Evaluating Suicide Education Courses

In an attempt to prevent teen suicide, many schools through-out the country have established suicide prevention courses. While these courses vary in format and length, they usually all provide information concerning the warning signs of suicide, and provide students with information on how to deal with someone who is suicidal. In addition, such courses may teach students coping techniques to help them deal with their prob-lems more effectively as a way of preventing depression and suicide.

These courses, however, are controversial. Many parents and educators believe such courses lead students to contemplate sui-cide, and possibly to kill themselves. Some opponents of suicide prevention courses also argue that suicide is too traumatic a topic for young people to confront, and that such courses only harm students emotionally.

This activity is designed to encourage discussion about the possible benefits and harms of suicide prevention courses. Consider these two opposing viewpoints on the topic:

Viewpoint I

Suicide ranks as the second leading cause of death among those between the ages of fifteen and twenty-four. Some 5,399 young people between the ages of five and twenty-four took their own lives in 1985, and many experts believe that figure would climb higher if suicides were reported accurately. Researchers estimate there are 100 to 120 attempts for each completed suicide.

Concerns about such figures have spawned a wide range of school programs aimed at suicide prevention. . . . The proper role of schools is to identify youths who may need professional intervention. . . . Soundly designed programs increase the like-lihood that connections will be made between caring adults and high-risk teenagers—and it is just possible that lives may be saved as a result.

In addition to their classroom component, comprehensive pro-grams include the following elements: crisis-intervention team training; teacher inservice training; parent workshops; contin-gency plans for dealing with a completed suicide; committees that work to form a community network for providing services to high-risk students and their families. . . . With suicide prevention as their object and identification of adolescent pathology as their primary strategy, integrated programs can become the most effective means for helping young people. . . .

Self-destructiveness among young people is a sign of the times that is not going to magically disappear. Only when children's well-being becomes a higher priority in our society—and not just in schools—will the war against such behavior be won.

We must begin to isolate those biological and environmental aspects of children's lives that may cause them to become self-destructive and try to change them. But until we can move forward on this course, comprehensive intervention programs offer a first line of defense and send a message to our young people that we care about them.

Thomas C. Barrett, *Education Week*, November 22, 1989. Reprinted with permission.

Viewpoint II

Two separate new studies have just concluded that suicide curricula in the schools and made-for-television movies about teen suicide do more harm than good. The evidence produced by these two research projects knocks the props out from under one of the psychological courses that has been a trendy fad in the public schools. . . .

According to a Columbia University study reported in the December 26, 1990 *Journal of the American Medical Association*, researchers led by Dr. David Shaffer found that the school courses stir up suicidal feelings when teenagers discuss the topic openly. Teenagers continued to believe that suicide was a possible solution to their problems, and those who took the course said that "talking about suicide makes some kids more likely to try to kill themselves." The researchers concluded that "There is a clear need to evaluate such programs to determine their efficacy and safety." The courses produced "unwanted effects" and the results are seen as a "cause for concern." . . .

The suicide and "death and dying" courses given in so many public schools today deal with the subject by having a counselor who has had only six to ten hours of training lead discussions in a classroom setting. The courses are based on the unproven concepts that suicide is caused by typical teenage stresses and that all teenagers share a potential vulnerability to suicide.

But most teenagers are *not* at risk for suicide and it is dangerous to pretend they are and expose them to classroom discussions about suicide. The Columbia study concluded that, because of the negative reactions to the suicide courses plus the evidence of "imitative or stimulatory effect on suicidal behavior" among adolescents, "the practice of addressing such programs to unselected audiences should be viewed with caution."

Dr. Shaffer warns that "suicide can be subject to imitation"

171

and that since, in any group, an unknown number of teens is pre-suicidal, talking about suicide could be "playing with fire." Telling them that "almost everyone has thought about suicide" tends to legitimize it. Several "cluster suicides" are a matter of record. . . .

Psychotherapy about a sensitive and volatile subject such as suicide, administered to a class of minor children (each with different emotional makeup) by a "counselor" (i.e., an unlicensed psychologist) who has spent a few hours in a workshop, should be prohibited in the public school classroom. It is to be hoped that legislatures and schools will now abandon their folly about suicide education.

Phyllis Schlafly, *The Phyllis Schlafly Report*, February 1991. Reprinted with permission.

Either by yourself or in a group, answer the following questions:

1. Do you believe schools should teach suicide prevention courses to teenagers? Why or why not?

2. Some people believe that schools have a responsibility to discuss issues such as death and suicide with students. Others believe that such topics are sensitive and personal, and should be reserved for discussion at home with parents. What do you think the schools' role should be? What do you think parents' role should be? Explain your reasoning.

3. Should there be an age limit for suicide education so that younger children are not exposed to it? If so, what should the age limit be?

4. Which of the above viewpoints do you think is more persuasive? Why? Did the viewpoints lead you to change your opinion?

Periodical Bibliography

The following articles have been selected to supplement the diverse views presented in this chapter.

Sandra R. Arbetter	"Recognizing the Signs of Suicide," *Current Health*, March 1987.
Ted Delaney	"Confronting Hopelessness at Wind River," *Utne Reader*, January/February 1990.
Thomas K. Edwards	"Providing Reasons for Wanting to Live," *Phi Delta Kappan*, December 1988.
Stanley L. Engelbardt	"It Can Be Prevented," *Reader's Digest*, July 1987.
Pam Feinour	"A High School Play Helps Suicidal Teenagers," *The Education Digest*, May 1989.
Jack Rimmel Frymier	"Understanding and Preventing Teen Suicide," *Phi Delta Kappan*, December 1988.
The Futurist	"Preventing Elderly Suicide," September/October 1991.
Eleanor Guetzloe	"School Prevention of Suicide, Violence, and Abuse," *The Education Digest*, February 1989.
Judy Lynn Hedberg	"I Don't Want to Live Anymore!" *Christian Social Action*, September 1989. Available from 100 Maryland Ave. NE, Washington, DC 20002.
Marianne Macy	"Lives on the Line," *New York*, April 22, 1991.
Jane Marks	"We Have a Problem," *Parents*, January 1989.
Parents	"Teen Suicide—The Warning Signs," January 1988.
Parents	"When Teens Talk Suicide," April 1989.
Prevention	"Magnesium: A Suicide-Prevention Mineral?" May 1987.
Science News	"Revising Short-Term Suicide Risks," September 20, 1990.
Maxine Seibel and Joseph N. Murray	"Early Prevention of Adolescent Suicide," *The Education Digest*, November 1988.
Edwin S. Shneidman	"At the Point of No Return," *Psychology Today*, March 1987.
Jane Wolfle	"Adolescent Suicide—An Open Letter to Counselors," *Phi Delta Kappan*, December 1988.

Organizations to Contact

The editors have compiled the following list of organizations that are concerned with the issues debated in this book. All have publications or information available for interested readers. For best results, allow as much time as possible for the organizations to respond. The descriptions below are derived from materials provided by the organizations. This list was compiled upon the date of publication. Names, addresses, and phone numbers of organizations are subject to change.

American Association of Suicidology
2459 S. Ash
Denver, CO 80222
(303) 692-0985

The association is one of the largest suicide prevention organizations in the nation. It believes that suicidal thoughts are almost always a symptom of depression and that suicide is almost never a rational decision. In addition to preventing suicide, the group also works to increase public awareness about suicide and to help those grieving the death of a loved one to suicide. The association publishes numerous pamphlets and reports.

American Life League (ALL)
PO Box 1350
Stafford, VA 22554
(703) 659-4171

ALL is a pro-life organization that provides books, pamphlets, and other educational materials to organizations opposed to abortion and physician-assisted suicide. Its publications include pamphlets, reports, and the monthly newsletter *ALL About Issues.*

Association for Death Education and Counseling (ADEC)
638 Prospect Ave.
Hartford, CT 06105-4298
(203) 232-4825

ADEC is an interdisciplinary organization that addresses dying, death, and bereavement issues from the educator's and counselor's perspective. It teaches educators, physicians, counselors, hospice personnel, clergy, and social workers how to counsel the grieving, the suicidal, and those who have lost a loved one to suicide. The association publishes the journal *Death Studies* and the newsletter *The Forum.*

Call for Help, Suicide, and Crisis Intervention
9400 Lebanon Rd.
Edgemont, IL 62203
crisis phone 1: (618) 397-0963
crisis phone 2: (618) 397-0964
crisis phone 3: (618) 397-0992
business phone: (618) 397-0968

Call for Help attempts to prevent suicide through crisis counseling and public education. It provides materials on suicide and suicide prevention upon request.

Center for Biomedical Ethics Publications
3-110 Owre Hall
UMHC Box 33
Harvard St. and E. River Rd.
Minneapolis, MN 55455

The center studies the ethical implications of biomedical practices such as organ transplantation, fetal tissue research, euthanasia, and physician-assisted suicide. It publishes reading packets that provide introductory overviews to specific topics. Each packet includes a discussion of the topic's central issues, articles, a bibliography, additional reading materials, and a forecast of future debate on the topic. Packet titles include *Withholding or Withdrawing Artificial Nutrition and Hydration, Termination of Treatment of Adults,* and *Individual Responsibility for Health.* In addition, the center publishes articles, books, and reports.

The Center for the Rights of the Terminally Ill (CRTI)
PO Box 54246
Hurst, TX 76054
(817) 656-5143

CRTI is an educational, patient advocacy, and political action organization that opposes assisted suicide and euthanasia. Its main purpose is to ensure that the sick and dying receive professional, competent, and ethical health care. The center works to achieve this goal through education and legislative action. It publishes the *CRTI Report* quarterly.

Community Connections
202-10534 124 St.
Edmonton, AB T5N 1S1
Canada
crisis phone: (403) 482-4357
business phone: (403) 482-0198

Community Connections is a crisis center that counsels those who are suicidal and depressed. In addition to its crisis hotline, the center sponsors community programs that address suicide prevention. Community Connections provides brochures and other publications to the public upon request.

The Compassionate Friends (TCF)
PO Box 3696
Oak Brook, IL 60522-3696
(708) 990-0010

TCF is an informal self-help organization for parents who have experienced the death of a child. It sponsors support group meetings, publishes brochures, and distributes books on parental and sibling grief, including *We Need Not Walk Alone.*

The Crisis and Information Center
101 W. Muhammad Ali Blvd.
Louisville, KY 40202
crisis phone 1: (502) 589-4313
TDD: (502) 589-4259
in Kentucky: (800) 221-0446
fax: (502) 589-8756
business phone: (502) 589-8630

The center responds to those who call or write for counseling or crisis intervention. In addition, it provides resources on suicide, suicide prevention, and crisis intervention to the public.

CRISIS Team
PO Box 85524
San Diego, CA 92186-5524
crisis phone 1: (619) 236-3339
San Diego County only: (800) 479-3339
business phone: (619) 692-8040

Through its crisis hotlines, the team offers counseling to the suicidal and those in need of emotional support. It also provides written materials to educate the public concerning suicide, suicide prevention, and crisis intervention.

Fairbanks Crisis Line
PO Box 70908
Fairbanks, AK 99707
crisis phone 1: (907) 452-4357
crisis phone 2: (907) 452-4403
business phone: (907) 451-8600

The crisis line provides counseling and compassion to those who are suicidal or facing a crisis. In addition to its crisis hotlines, the center provides information to the public concerning suicide prevention. It provides books, pamphlets, and other materials to the public upon request.

Father Flanagan's Boys' Home
Town Hall
Boys' Town, NE 68010
Boys' Town National Hotline: (800) 448-3000
business phone: (402) 498-1830

Father Flanagan's Boys' Home was established in 1917 as a home for troubled or orphaned boys. Since then, it has grown in size and in the scope of its mission, which now includes providing counseling to troubled and suicidal teens. The home provides the public with pamphlets and other materials concerning teen crisis and suicide.

Foundation II, Inc.
1540 Second Ave. SE
Cedar Rapids, IA 52403
crisis phone: (319) 362-2174
in Iowa: (800) 332-4224

The foundation's primary goal is to assist suicidal and despondent individuals and to educate the public concerning suicide. The organization provides information, including pamphlets and brochures, to the public on suicide and suicide prevention.

The Foundation of Thanatology
630 W. 168th St.
New York, NY 10032
(212) 928-2066

This organization of health, theology, psychology, and social science professionals is devoted to scientific and humanist inquiries into death, loss, grief, and bereavement. The foundation, formed in 1967, coordinates professional, educational, and research programs concerned with mortality and grief. It publishes the periodicals *Advances in Thanatology* and *Archives of the Foundation of Thanatology*.

The Hastings Center
255 Elm Rd.
Briarcliff Manor, NY 10510
(914) 762-8500

Since its founding in 1969, the Hastings Center has addressed the ethical implications of medical practices such as euthanasia and assisted suicide. The center's goals are to promote research on the issues, to stimulate universities to support the teaching of ethics, and to educate the public. It publishes the *Hastings Center Report* bimonthly.

The Hemlock Society
PO Box 11830
Eugene, OR 97440-3900
(503) 342-5748

The society supports the practice of voluntary suicide by the terminally ill and believes that the final decision to terminate one's life is one's own. It does not encourage suicide for anyone who is not terminally ill, and it supports suicide prevention programs. It publishes books on suicide, death, and dying, including *Final Exit*, a guide to those who are suffering with terminal illnesses and considering suicide. The society also publishes the *Hemlock Quarterly*.

Jewish Family Service
2026 St. Charles
New Orleans, LA 70130
(504) 524-8475

Jewish Family Service works to educate the public concerning suicide, suicide prevention, and dealing with personal and family crises. To accomplish this goal, it sponsors educational programs and provides materials upon request.

LETS—Let's End Teen Suicide
621 S. New Ballas, Suite 4018, Tower B
St. Louis, MO 63141
(314) 432-5387

LETS works to educate the public about teen suicide and to find ways to prevent teens from taking their lives. It sponsors programs and provides information to the public upon request.

Life Crisis Services, Inc.
1423 S. Big Bend Blvd.
St. Louis, MO 63117
adults: (314) 647-4357
teens: (314) 644-5886
business phone: (314) 647-3100

Life Crisis Services, Inc., offers counseling and emotional support to adults and teenagers who are facing personal crises and who may be suicidal. The organization provides materials on suicide and suicide prevention to the public upon request.

National Right to Life
419 Seventh St. NW, Suite 500
Washington, DC 20004-2293
phone: (202) 626-8800
fax: (202) 737-9189

National Right to Life opposes abortion, euthanasia, and physician-assisted suicide because it believes these practices disregard the value of human life. The group organizes protests at the national and local level and publishes many articles, pamphlets, and reports to promote its position. Its *National Right to Life News* is published twice a month.

Pinellas Emergency MHS, Inc.
11254 58th St. N
Pinellas Park, FL 34666-2606
crisis phone 1: (813) 791-3131
crisis phone 2: (813) 791-1117
business phone: (813) 545-5636

Pinellas Emergency MHS, Inc., is a suicide prevention service. Through its crisis hotlines and outreach to the public, it attempts to prevent suicide and provide counseling to those in distress. The organization has a packet of publications available upon request.

Samaritans
500 Commonwealth Ave.
Kenmore Sq.
Boston, MA 02215
(617) 247-0220

Samaritans is the largest suicide prevention organization in the world. Established in England in 1953, the organization now has branches in at least forty-four nations throughout the world. The group's volunteers counsel the suicidal and provide assistance in other ways to help the despondent. In addition, Samaritans provides pamphlets, reports, and other publications to the public.

SAVE—Suicide Awareness/Voices of Education
c/o Adina Wrobleski
PO Box 24507
Minneapolis, MN 55424
(612) 871-0068

SAVE is a bereavement organization that works to help those grieving after the suicide of a loved one. It also strives to educate the public about suicide. In addition to pamphlets and the book *Suicide: Survivors—A Guide for Those Left Behind*, the organization publishes the quarterly newsletter *Afterwords*.

Seasons: Suicide Bereavement
c/o Tina Larson
PO Box 187
Perk City, UT 84060
(801) 649-8327

Seasons is a self-help organization for people who have lost a family member or friend to suicide. The group provides an opportunity for such people to express the emotional pain, guilt, and anger often associated with suicide bereavement. The group's leader also helps others start their own groups. Seasons publishes pamphlets on suicide bereavement.

Suicide and Crisis Center
PO Box 3250
Amarillo, TX 79116-3250
crisis phone 1: (806) 359-6699
in Texas: (800) 692-4039
teenline: (806) 353-2255
business phone: (806) 353-0097

The Suicide and Crisis Center provides a variety of services to those facing personal crisis. In addition to its crisis hotline, which provides counseling to the suicidal and others, the center also provides assistance to teenagers and children who need help in dealing with emotional problems. The center provides written materials on suicide, suicide prevention, and crisis intervention upon request.

Suicide Prevention/Crisis Intervention
PO Box 9102
Berkeley, CA 94709
crisis phone: (510) 849-2212
business phone: (510) 848-1515

Suicide Prevention/Crisis Intervention is a suicide and crisis center that provides counseling and compassion to those who need emotional support. It provides brochures, pamphlets, and other materials to the public upon request.

University of Pittsburgh School of Nursing
c/o Rose E. Constantino or Ann M. Mitchell
414 Victoria Bldg.
Pittsburgh, PA 15261
(412) 624-9005

The School of Nursing sponsors a project that studies and helps those who have lost a loved one to suicide. The school provides referrals to those seeking help. It publishes two bibliographies on suicide in addition to other resources.

Yad Tikvah Foundation
c/o Union of American Hebrew Congregations
1330 Beacon St., Rm. 355
Brookline, MA 02146
(617) 277-1655

The foundation works to prevent youth suicide. It works with Jewish congregations and schools to educate students, teachers, and parents about the warning signs of suicide and ways to prevent it. The foundation provides pamphlets and other materials to the public upon request.

Annotated Book Bibliography

Alcohol, Drug Abuse, and Mental Health Administration
Report of the Secretary's Task Force on Youth Suicide. Washington, DC: Superintendent of Documents, U.S. Government Printing Office, 1989. A four-volume report that provides an overview of youth suicide in America, discusses possible causes of teen suicide, and suggests strategies for suicide prevention.

Robert M. Baird and Stuart E. Rosenbaum, eds.
Euthanasia: The Moral Issues. Buffalo: Prometheus Books, 1989. This balanced anthology presents a variety of views on euthanasia and assisted suicide. Contributing authors include moral theorists and physicians such as Sidney H. Wanzer, C. Everett Koop, Leon R. Kass, and Gerald A. Larue.

John Q. Baucom
Fatal Choice: The Teenage Suicide Crisis. Chicago: Moody Press, 1986. The author, a Christian psychologist, offers practical, professional advice to parents and peers of teens who are troubled, depressed, and suicidal.

Arnold R. Beisser
A Graceful Passage: Notes on the Freedom to Live or Die. New York: Doubleday, 1990. The author, who has lived in an iron lung for many years, discusses the meaning of life and death and the individual's right to choose how to live and how to die.

Alan L. Berman and David A. Jobes
Adolescent Suicide: Assessment and Intervention. Washington, DC: American Psychological Association, 1991. The authors use case examples to illustrate possible causes of teen suicide and thoroughly examine the benefits and liabilities of prevention programs. The book is a comprehensive guide to the facts and beliefs concerning teen suicide.

Iris Bolten
My Son . . . My Son. Atlanta: Bolten Press, 1987. Bolten describes her grieving process after the suicide of her son. Her story offers guidance and hope to others who have suffered the suicide of a loved one.

Baruch Brody
Life and Death Decision Making. New York: Oxford University Press, 1988. Brody, a professor of biomedical ethics and philosophy, describes forty ethical dilemmas physicians face, including the dilemma of physician-assisted suicide of the terminally ill. Brody offers a problem-solving framework for each dilemma and discusses how theoretical views of life and death relate to dying and dealing with patients' wishes to die.

California Department of Mental Health
The California Helper's Handbook for Suicide Prevention. Sacramento: California Department of Mental Health, 1990. A guide for those interested in preventing suicide. The handbook suggests ways to recognize someone who is suicidal and how to respond appropriately.

Robert Campbell and Diane Collinson
Ending Lives. Oxford, England: Basil Blackwell, 1988. The authors ponder the moral problems presented by suicide and euthanasia, and compare the value of dying compared to the vaue of living.

Peter Cimbolic and David A. Jobes, eds.	*Youth Suicide: Issues, Assessment, and Intervention.* Springfield, IL: Charles C Thomas, 1990. This book discusses ways to anticipate and prevent teen suicide and analyzes the effectiveness of prevention programs.
James T. Clemons	*What Does the Bible Say About Suicide?* Minneapolis: Fortress Press, 1990. In this volume, the author reviews biblical teachings applicable to suicide and offers guidance on how to respond compassionately to friends and relatives of those who have committed suicide.
James T. Clemons, ed.	*Sermons on Suicide.* Louisville: Westminster/John Knox Press, 1989. This anthology presents sermons by theologians who explore suicide issues from a Christian perspective. Among the issues addressed are the problem of the unendurable physical or emotional pain that leads to suicide, whether suicide is a sin, and whether individuals should have the right to kill themselves.
George Howe Colt	*The Enigma of Suicide.* New York: Summit Books, 1991. In a very readable style, the author presents the true stories of several suicide victims and their families. Interspersed with the stories are chapters on the history of suicide and suicide prevention, the causes of suicide, and the debate concerning the effectiveness of suicide hotlines.
John Donnelly, ed.	*Suicide: Right or Wrong?* Buffalo: Prometheus Books, 1990. Donnelly's anthology presents arguments supporting and opposing suicide from such renowned authors as Seneca, Thomas Aquinas, David Hume, Immanuel Kant, Edwin S. Shneidman, Thomas S. Szasz, and Joyce Carol Oates.
Carlos Gomez	*Regulating Death: Euthanasia and the Case of the Netherlands.* New York: The Free Press, 1991. The Netherlands is often cited as one of the few nations that allows physician-assisted suicide. American physician Carlos Gomez investigated the practice of euthanasia in the Netherlands and presents his discoveries in this book. While Gomez does not directly oppose assisted suicide, his description of the cases he studied clearly shows that he questions whether the Dutch have thoughtfully considered the implications of the practice. Gomez recounts the assisted suicides of patients who are not terminally ill and of retarded infants who could be treated but whose parents refuse to approve life-saving treatment. The book's foreword is written by Leon R. Kass, a physician who vehemently opposes assisted suicide.
Barbara Barrett Hicks	*Youth Suicide: A Comprehensive Manual for Prevention and Intervention.* Bloomington, IN: National Educational Service, 1990. A guide to detecting and responding to the warning signs of suicidal tendencies in youth. The book includes a training program for suicide prevention volunteers.

181

Douglas Jacobs and Herbert N. Brown, eds.	*Suicide: Understanding and Responding*. Madison, CT: International Universities Press, 1989. In this thorough volume, the editors provide a variety of views on suicide, including perspectives on the causes of suicide, the problems in recognizing and responding to suicidal behavior, and the moral implications of suicide. The volume includes the views of many experts on suicide such as Karl Menninger, Thomas S. Szasz, and Edwin S. Shneidman.
Derek Humphrey	*Final Exit: The Practicality of Self-Deliverance and Assisted Suicide for the Dying.* Eugene, OR: The Hemlock Society, 1991. This controversial, best-selling book by the founder of the Hemlock Society supports the individual's right to die and provides information on various ways to commit suicide.
Jack Kevorkian	*Prescription: Medicide: The Goodness of Planned Death.* Buffalo: Prometheus Books, 1991. Kevorkian, a physician, has been at the center of the right-to-die debate because of his participation in the suicides of several people in Michigan. In his book, he describes his reasons for helping others commit suicide and defends his belief that suicide is an individual's right. Kevorkian proposes that suicide and assisted suicide be legalized and that society establish *obitoriums*, or suicide centers, where people can commit suicide legally and painlessly.
Howard I. Kushner	*Self-Destruction in the Promised Land: A Psychocultural Biology of American Suicide.* New Brunswick, NJ: Rutgers University Press, 1989. In this sociological overview of suicide, Kushner details suicide in America from the time of the Puritans to today. He analyzes Americans' attitudes about suicide and the nation's various attempts to prevent suicide. Interspersed throughout the book are the stories of Americans, such as explorer Meriwether Lewis, who killed themselves.
Gerald A. Larue	*Euthanasia and Religion: A Survey of the Attitudes of World Religions to the Right-to-Die.* Eugene, OR: The Hemlock Society, 1985. Larue, a noted professor of religion and gerontology, presents a comprehensive overview, in lay terms, of the positions of the world's major religions concerning the individual's right to die.
Antoon A. Leenaars	*Suicide Notes.* New York: Human Sciences Press, 1987. Leenaars, a well-known expert on suicide, analyzes the case studies and suicide notes of people who have killed themselves. Through his analyses, the author attempts to understand why people commit suicide. An appendix includes a selection of authentic suicide notes.
Michael R. Leming and George E. Dickinson	*Understanding Dying, Death, and Bereavement.* 2d ed. Fort Worth, TX: Holt, Rinehart, and Winston, 1990. The authors, professors of sociology, have taught courses on death and dying for many years. In this textbook, they evaluate attitudes toward death, dying, and grief. Entire chapters discuss the possible causes of suicide, the warning signs of suicide, suicide in teenagers and the elderly, and suicide prevention.

David Lester	*Understanding and Preventing Suicide: New Perspectives.* Springfield, IL: Charles C Thomas, 1990. Lester, a psychology professor and author of several books on suicide, outlines a variety of sociological theories on suicide, including those of Emile Durkheim, Thorsten Sellin, and others. In his analysis, he discusses the rationality of suicide, the legality of suicide, the relationships between the suicidal and their families and society, and suicide prevention.
Michael Miller with Debra Whalley Kidney	*Dare to Live: A Guide to the Understanding and Prevention of Teenage Suicide and Depression.* Hillsboro, OR: Beyond Words Publishing, 1989. The authors relate case studies of teen suicides and attempted suicides in an effort to inform teachers, parents, and peers about teen depression and suicide.
Richard W. Momeyer	*Confronting Death.* Bloomington: Indiana University Press, 1988. Momeyer, a professor at Miami University of Ohio, discusses the meaning of death and dying and ponders the philosophical problems of suicide. While he believes that society should do everything it can to support people in times of crisis and that it should attempt to prevent suicide, he believes that suicide is ultimately an individual right.
Cynthia R. Pfeffer, ed.	*Suicide Among Youth: Perspectives on Risk and Prevention.* Washington, DC: American Psychiatric Press, 1989. Pfeffer has compiled an anthology representing the views of many physicians, psychologists, and sociologists concerning youth suicide. The contributors discuss the psychological characteristics of suicidal teens; possible ways to predict suicide; and the role of the family, genetics, the media, and peers in youth suicide. The volume also analyzes the effectiveness of suicide prevention measures.
Tonia K. Shamoo and Philip G. Patros	*"I Want to Kill Myself": Helping Your Child Cope with Depression and Suicidal Thoughts.* New York: Lexington Books, 1990. This guide teaches parents to recognize symptoms of depression so they can prevent suicide in their children.
Judith M. Stillion, Eugene E. McDowell, and Jacque H. May	*Suicide Across the Life Span: Premature Exits.* New York: Hemisphere Publishing Corp., 1989. A comprehensive sociological overview of suicide. The authors discuss suicide among all age groups, present perspectives on the various causes of suicide, and evaluate the effectiveness of suicide prevention measures.
William Styron	*Darkness Visible: A Memoir of Madness.* New York: Random House, 1990. In this autobiographical account, the well-known author of such acclaimed novels as *Sophie's Choice* and *The Confessions of Nat Turner* describes his descent into depression, his contemplation of suicide, and his subsequent recovery.
James J. Walter and Thomas A. Shannon, eds.	*Quality of Life: The New Medical Dilemma.* New York: Paulist Press, 1990. The editors have compiled a balanced, thorough collection of articles and guidelines for understanding the phrase "quality of life" that is commonly used today as society confronts the issue

of the right of the terminally or chronically ill to commit suicide. The anthology includes both secular and theological articles that discuss the controversies of assisted suicide and euthanasia.

Robert N. Wennberg

Terminal Choices: Euthanasia, Suicide, and the Right to Die. Grand Rapids, MI: William B. Eerdmans, 1989. This volume thoroughly discusses the issues of suicide and euthanasia. It explains historical attitudes concerning suicide and includes several chapters on the definition and morality of suicide and euthanasia. The author concludes that both suicide and euthanasia should be opposed.

Ann Wickett

Double Exit: When Aging Couples Commit Suicide Together. Eugene, OR: The Hemlock Society, 1989. The elderly have the highest rate of suicide of any age group in America. In this volume, the author relates the stories of elderly couples who have committed suicide together. Wickett analyzes these cases and the reasons so many of the elderly commit suicide.

Adina Wrobleski

Suicide: Survivors—A Guide for Those Left Behind. Minneapolis: Afterwords, 1991. A self-help manual for people who were close to someone who committed suicide. The author discusses problems faced by survivors, including their own guilt and anger and the blame given them by society. She suggests how to deal with these issues and lists resources available to survivors.

Index

acquired immunodeficiency
syndrome (AIDS), 58, 104, 107
Alabama, 134
Alberta, Canada, 96
alcohol use, 144
can cause suicide, 94-99, 104-105
Alessi, N., 97-98
American Association of Suicidology,
141, 142, 147, 159
American Medical Association, 33,
52, 59
Americans Against Human Suffering,
34, 36
Aristotle, 19
Asay, Chuck, 60
Austria, 118
autonomy, personal, 20, 27-29, 59

Bell, Alan P., 101
Benson, Steve, 40
Berkovitz, Irving, 110
Berman, Alan L., 82, 143
Bettelheim, Bruno, 36
Bible, 26, 71, 112
blacks, 115, 156
Brent, David A., 88

California, 52
Callahan, Daniel, 69
Canada, 93, 95-96, 141
cancer, 64
Cantor, Pamela, 110, 117, 142
capital punishment, 71
carbon monoxide, 66
Carlson, Allan C., 108
Carroll, T., 82
Catrow, Dave, 33
Charen, Mona, 29
Charen, Walter D., 29
Churchill, Winston S., 43
"cluster" suicides, 86
Colt, George Howe, 110, 112, 114,
127, 149
common law, 25, 29, 55, 65, 70
Corder, B., 154
courts, 34-35, 52, 54
Crime Prevention Coalition, 149

Davidson, L., 146, 147
DeBlassie, Richard, 110
Declaration of Independence, 28, 37
Deerhunter, The, 146-147
depression

as cause of suicide, 28, 29, 84, 165
in adolescents, 28, 84
in elderly, 165, 166-167, 168
in terminal illness, 30, 55
treatment of, 30, 55, 60-61, 166-
167, 168
divorce, 153, 154
rates of, 111, 112, 113
Donnelly, John, 118
do-not-resuscitate (DNR) orders, 52
Douglas, Stephen A., 27-28
drug abuse
can cause suicide, 94-99, 104-105
Durkheim, Emile, 111, 152, 155
Duszynski, K., 153

education, 148
can prevent suicide, 135-142
Eisenberg, Leon, 149
elderly, 90
suicide prevention, 154, 162-169
Elkind, David, 83
Ely, Margot, 109
Epstein, L., 154
Erikson, Erik H., 84, 138
euthanasia, 22, 27
in the Netherlands, 58, 66
laws prohibiting, 26, 34, 35, 65,
71-72
physican involvement in, 55, 58
is ethical, 63, 64, 65, 66, 67-68
con, 59, 70, 71, 73-74, 75
should be legalized, 65
con, 70, 72-73

families
as cause of suicide, 108-113,
152-153
can prevent suicide, 113, 154, 156
Final Exit (Humphry), 39
Finland, 164
Flay, B.R., 147, 148
Fletcher, Joseph, 34-35
Forsythe, Clarke D., 24
Frederick, Calvin, 110,
Freud, Sigmund, 36, 83, 84
friends, 153
can prevent suicide, 158-161

Gallup Poll, 53
Ganzler, S., 152
Garfinkel, B., 97
Gibson, Paul, 100

Gock, T., 101
Goethe, Johann Wolfgang von, 146
Goldstein, H.K., 147
Gorowitz, Samuel, 64
Gould, Madelyn, 146, 147, 149
Great Depression, 166
Greenberg, B., 144
Greuling, Jacquelin, 110
guns
  cause suicide, 88-93
  laws controlling, 89, 92, 93

Hamrick, Kimberly R., 140
Harvard Law Review, 25
Hemlock Society, 34, 36
Hippocrates, 59, 63
Hippocratic oath, 63
homosexuality
  social stigma against causes
    suicide, 100-107
Hong Kong, 165
hospices, 23
Houk, Vernon N., 90, 92
human rights, 18, 22, 23
Humphry, Derek, 26-27, 39, 40, 41,
  42
Huntley, S., 144

illnesses, 165

Jacobs, J., 152-153
Jay, Karla, 101
Jefferson, Thomas, 37
Johnson, Alan W., 31
Johnson, B.D., 152

Kalasardo, Beverly, 132
Kamisar, Yale, 59
Kant, Immanuel, 42-43
Kaplan, H., 153
Kass, Leon R., 38, 61
Kelson v. City of Springfield, Oregon
  (1985), 138-139
Kennedy, H., 144
Kevorkian, Jack, 62, 71
Klugman, David, 134
Koran, 26, 71
Kraai, John, 65

LaFontaine, David, 105
Larkin Street Youth Center
  (San Francisco), 104-105
Lester, David, 113, 151, 152, 154
Lincoln, Abraham, 27-28
Litman, Robert, 119-120, 134
living wills, 26, 52
Los Angeles Suicide Prevention
  Center (LASPC)

gay youth study, 104, 105
public service announcements, 147
suicide prevention efforts, 128,
  129-130, 131-132, 133
Louisville, Ky., 95

McDowell, Eugene E., 81, 135, 167
McGuire, Donald, 109
Mack, John, 117
Madigan, Tim, 36
Maguen, Shira, 102
Mandelkorn, Philip, 129, 131
Maris, Ronald W., 133, 153
mass media
  can prevent suicide, 143-150
May, Jacque H., 81, 135, 167
Means, Cyril, 25
medical treatment
  right to refuse, 25, 26, 52, 53, 59,
    61
mental illness, 28, 160
Mercy, James A., 90, 92
Model Suicide Assistance Statute, 30
Momeyer, Richard W., 17
Morgan, Alexander C., 162
Motto, Jerome, 133
murder, 65, 66, 119

National Gay Task Force, 101
National Institute of Mental Health
  (NIMH), 144
Native Americans, 115
Netherlands, 34, 58, 66
Neuringer, C., 153
New Haven, Conn., 95
New York Native, 105
New York Times, 145
Nietzsche, Friedrich, 134
Nolan, Joseph R., 28
nursing homes, 53-54

Oates, Joyce Carol, 42
"obitiatry," 67-68
Orentlicher, David, 57

pain relief, 54, 74
parent-teacher association (PTA),
  142
Patel, A., 97
Peck, Michael, 116
personality disorder, 99
Pett, Joel, 64
Pfeffer, Cynthia, 109
Phillips, David P., 145, 146
physicians
  suicide assistance and
    is ethical, 29-30, 34, 51-56
    con, 30, 57-61

should be legal, 37, 62-68
    con, 69-75
suicide prevention and, 92, 93
Piaget, Jean, 86
Plato, 19
Plotkin, Daniel, 28
Pokorny, A.D., 153
Portwood, Doris, 35
privacy rights, 25, 26-27, 39, 52
property rights, 18, 19-20
Protestants, 111
psychotherapy, 156-157
public service announcements
    (PSAs), 147-148, 149

Radecki, T., 146-147
rational choice
    suicide can be, 31-37, 55, 56
        con, 27, 28, 29, 30, 38-43, 60-61
religion
    and homosexuality, 103-104
    and right to suicide, 19, 21, 42
    deecline of causes suicide, 108-113
Richman, Joseph, 156
right to die, 22, 23, 25, 26, 39
Robbins, D., 97-98
rock music, 147
Roethke, Theodore, 82
Roe v. Wade (1973), 26-27
Rofes, Eric E., 102
Rogers, Carl, 131
Rosenberg, Mark L., 90, 92, 115
Rosenblum, Victor G., 24
Ross, Charlotte, 109, 110
Rubinstein, E.A., 146

Sacco, V.F., 148
Samaritans, The, 85, 134
San Francisco Suicide Prevention,
    134
schools, 155-156
    suicide prevention programs, 110,
    137, 138-142
Schuckit, Judith J., 94
Schuckit, Marc A., 94
Schur, Max, 36
Seattle, Wash., 89
self-defense,
    killing in, 71
self-esteem, 84, 153, 169
sexuality, 83-84
Shaffer, David, 149
Shafii, M., 97
Shneidman, Edwin S., 117, 129, 131,
    160
Silverman, R.A., 148
Smith, Kim, 115-116
Sobel, J.L., 148

social bonds
    can prevent suicide, 151-157
Society for the Right to Die, 58
Sorrows of Young Werther (Goethe),
    146
Spoonhour, Anne, 110
Spoonhour, Justin, 110
Stack, Steven, 111-112
Stark, Rodney, 112
states
    homosexuality prohibitions in, 101-
    102
    living will laws, 26, 52
    suicide assistance laws, 25, 26, 55,
    65-66
    suicide prevention programs, 139
Steinem, Gloria, 32, 34
Stillion, Judith M., 81, 135, 167
stress
    as cause of teen suicide, 81-87
suicide
    as an individual right, 17-23
        con, 24-30
    assisted
        by a physician
            as ethical, 29-30, 34, 51-56
                con, 30, 57-61
        laws prohibiting, 25, 26, 34, 35,
        55, 58
        should be legal, 62-68
            con, 69-75
    attempts, 85, 95, 109, 115-116, 159
    can be a rational choice, 31-37, 55,
    56
        con, 27, 28, 29, 30, 38-43, 60, 61
    depression causes, 28, 29, 84, 165
    prevention methods
        crisis centers, 23, 127-134,
        156-157, 161
        educating friends, 158-161
        education, 135-142
        improving the lives of the elderly,
        154
        increasing social bonds, 151-157
        using mass media, 143-150
    rates, 134, 149
        for children, 109
        for elderly, 163, 164-165, 167
        for teens, 95, 115, 118
        in the United States, 95-96, 159,
        163, 164, 165
        per attempt, 85, 95, 115-116, 159
    threats, 85, 109, 159
"suicide centers," 67-68
Suicide Prevention and Crisis Center
    of San Mateo County, California,
    158
Survivors of Suicide (SOS), 142

187

Switzerland, 118
Szasz, Thomas S., 21
Talmud, 26, 71
teen suicide
  causes of, 114-120
    alcohol and drug abuse, 94-99
      104-105
    depression, 28, 84
    guns in the home, 88-93
    homosexuality, social stigma of,
      100-107
    religion and family decline, 108-
      113, 152-153, 154
    stress, 81-87
  prevention of, 136, 138, 142, 148
  television and, 144-145, 149
television, 144-146, 149
terminal illness, 37, 52, 54-55, 56, 72,
  73
Thomas, C., 153
Tifft, S., 156

Union Pacific v. Bostford (1891), 70

United States
  Department of Health and Human
    Services, 96, 116
  suicide prevention programs, 141
  suicide rates in, 95-96, 159, 163,
    164, 165
  Supreme Court, 70

Vancouver, B.C., 89
Vince, Cheryl J., 140

Wallack, L., 144
Wanzer, Sidney H., 29, 51
Washington Times, 26, 71
Wasserman, I., 146
Weinberg, Martin S., 101
Western Psychiatric Institute and
  Clinic (WPIC), 90
Wingspread Conference (1987), 142
Wood, Mark, 102
Wright, Don, 19

Young, Allen, 101